DATE DUE

FEB 24 '96			
AG 08 '97			
NO 20 '99			
AUG 22 05			
MY 15 '06			

The Library Store   #47-0102

Gary E. McCuen

IDEAS IN CONFLICT SERIES

publications inc.
502 Second Street
Hudson, Wisconsin 54016
Phone (715) 386-7113

Library of Congress Cataloging-in-Publication Data

McCuen, Gary E.
　　Religion and politics.

　　(Ideas in conflict)
　　Bibliography: p.
　　1. Religion and politics. 2. Freedom of religion. 3. Religious tolerance. 4. Church and state. 5. Church and education. I. McCuen, Gary E. II. Series.
BL65.P7R4326 1989　　　　　323.44′2　　　　　88-42848
ISBN 0-86596-069-0

Illustration & photo credits

Americans for Religious Liberty 160, Web Bryant 151, Herblock 120, Dan Hubig 147, Joel Kauffman 163, *Luther and the Jews* 27, 37, Geoffrey Moss 91, Bill Plympton 126, William Sanders 109, David Seavey 133, 140, Stein 113, Ron Swanson 17.

publications inc.　© 1989 by Gary E. McCuen Publications, Inc.
502 Second Street • Hudson, Wisconsin 54016
　　(715) 386-7113
International Standard Book Number 0-86596-069-0
Printed in the United States of America

CONTENTS

CHAPTER 3 RELIGION AND EDUCATION

CHAPTER 4 RELIGION AND PUBLIC POLICY

REASONING SKILL DEVELOPMENT

These activities may be used as individualized study guides for students in libraries and resource centers or as discussion catalysts in small group and classroom discussions.

IDEAS in CONFLICT ®

This series features ideas in conflict on political, social, and moral issues. It presents counterpoints, debates, opinions, commentary, and analysis for use in libraries and classrooms. Each title in the series uses one or more of the following basic elements:

Introductions that present an issue overview giving historic background and/or a description of the controversy.

Counterpoints and debates carefully chosen from publications, books, and position papers on the political right and left to help librarians and teachers respond to requests that treatment of public issues be fair and balanced.

Symposiums and forums that go beyond debates that can polarize and oversimplify. These present commentary from across the political spectrum that reflect how complex issues attract many shades of opinion.

A *global* emphasis with foreign perspectives and surveys on various moral questions and political issues that will help readers to place subject matter in a less culture-bound and ethnocentric frame of reference. In an ever-shrinking and interdependent world, understanding and cooperation are essential. Many issues are global in nature and can be effectively dealt with only by common efforts and international understanding.

Reasoning skill study guides and discussion activities provide ready-made tools for helping with critical reading and evaluation of content. The guides and activities deal with one or more of the following:

RECOGNIZING AUTHOR'S POINT OF VIEW

INTERPRETING EDITORIAL CARTOONS

VALUES IN CONFLICT

WHAT IS EDITORIAL BIAS?

WHAT IS SEX BIAS?

WHAT IS POLITICAL BIAS?

WHAT IS ETHNOCENTRIC BIAS?

WHAT IS RACE BIAS?

WHAT IS RELIGIOUS BIAS?

From across **the political spectrum** *varied sources are presented for research projects and classroom discussions. Diverse opinions in the series come from magazines, newspapers, syndicated columnists, books, political speeches, foreign nations, and position papers by corporations and nonprofit institutions.*

About the Editor

Gary E. McCuen is an editor and publisher of anthologies for public libraries and curriculum materials for schools. Over the past 18 years his publications of over 200 titles have specialized in social, moral, and political conflict. They include books, pamphlets, cassettes, tabloids, filmstrips, and simulation games, many of them designed from his curriculums during 11 years of teaching junior and senior high school social studies. At present he is the editor and publisher of the *Ideas in Conflict* series and the *Editorial Forum* series.

CHAPTER 1

RELIGIOUS INTOLERANCE THROUGHOUT HISTORY

1 RELIGIOUS INTOLERANCE THROUGHOUT HISTORY

RELIGION AND POLITICS: AN OVERVIEW

World Book Encyclopedia

The following reading provides an overview on the relationship between religion and politics and describes the nature of religious intolerance throughout history.

Richard E. Morgan, "Freedom of Religion," *The World Book Encyclopedia,* 1988 ed. volume 7, pp. 505-506. From *The World Book Encyclopedia.* © 1988 World Book, Inc.

Throughout most of history, many people have been persecuted for their religious beliefs. The denial of religious liberty probably stems from two major sources—personal and political. Religion touches the deepest feelings of many people. Strong religious views have led to intolerance among various faiths. Some governments have close ties to one religion and consider people of other faiths to be a threat to political authority. A government also may regard religion as politically dangerous because religions may place allegiance to God above obedience to the state.

The question of morality has caused many conflicts between church and state. Both religion and government are concerned with morality. They work together if the moral goals desired by the state are the same as those sought by the church. But discord may result if they have different views about morality. An example is the disagreement of many religious people with governments that allow abortion.

History

Many ancient peoples permitted broad religious freedom. These peoples worshipped many gods and readily accepted groups with new gods. Jews and, later, Christians could not do so because they worshipped only one God. They also believed that allegiance to God was higher than allegiance to any ruler or state. Some ancient peoples did not accept these beliefs, and they persecuted Christians and Jews.

During the Middle Ages, from about the A.D. 500s to the 1500s, the Catholic Church dominated Europe and permitted little religious freedom. The church persecuted Jews and Muslims. It punished people for any serious disagreement with its teachings. In 1415, the Bohemian religious reformer John Hus was burned at the stake for challenging the pope's authority.

The Reformation, a religious movement of the 1500s, gave birth to Protestantism. The Catholic Church and Catholic rulers persecuted Protestant groups. Many Protestant denominations persecuted Catholics and other Protestant groups as well. But by the 1700s and 1800s, the variety of religions that resulted from the Reformation had led to increased tolerance in many countries. These countries included Great Britain, the Netherlands, and the United States. But intolerance remained strong in some countries. Poland and Russia, for example, severely persecuted Jews. One of the most savage religious persecutions in history occurred in the 1930s and 1940s, when Nazi Germany killed about 6 million Jews.

In the United States

The desire for religious freedom was a major reason Europeans settled in America. The Puritans and many other groups came to the New World to escape religious persecution in Europe.

10

The First Amendment of the United States Constitution guarantees that "Congress shall make no law respecting an establishment of religion, or prohibiting the free exercise thereof. . . ." This provision originally protected religious groups from unfair treatment by the federal government only. Until the mid-1800s, New Hampshire and some other states had laws that prohibited non-Protestants from holding public office. Several states, including Connecticut and Massachusetts, even had official state churches. Since the 1940s, however, the Supreme Court of the United States has ruled that all of the states must uphold the First Amendment's guarantees of religious freedom.

Today, freedom of religion remains an issue in the United States. Various court rulings have interpreted the First Amendment to mean that the government may not promote or give special treatment to any religion. Judges have struck down plans that called for the government to give financial aid to religious schools. The courts have also ruled unconstitutional a number of programs to teach the Bible or recite prayers in public schools. These rulings are highly controversial.

But church and state are not completely separated in the United States. The nation's motto is *In God We Trust*. Sessions of Congress open with prayers, and court witnesses swear oaths on the Bible. Several court decisions support such practices.

Christian moral views have had a predominant influence on U.S. laws because most of the nation's people are Christians. In 1878, for example, the Supreme Court upheld a federal law against polygamy (the practice of having more than one wife or husband at the same time), even though this law restricted the religious freedom of one Christian group, the Mormons. At that time, the Mormon faith included belief in polygamy. But the laws and the courts agreed with the view of most Americans that polygamy is harmful to society.

In Other Countries

Religion has been discouraged or even forbidden in countries ruled by dictators. For example, the governments of China, the Soviet Union, and other Communist nations have persecuted religion on a large scale. A person's highest allegiance, they believe, belongs to Communism, not to a Supreme Being. Communist dictators consider religion a competitor for such allegiance. Although they do not forbid religion entirely, they make it difficult for people to practice any faith. Communist authorities have imprisoned religious leaders and have closed churches. The Soviet Union has conducted intensive propaganda campaigns to persuade people not to attend church. China has imprisoned or expelled foreign missionaries.

In some countries that have an official state church, or where most of the people belong to one church, other faiths do not have religious freedom. For example, many Muslim nations discriminate against Christians and Jews. Even in countries that do not have a state church, members of minority religions may have economic or social disadvantages. Roman Catholics in Northern Ireland, which is mostly Protestant, complain of such unfair treatment.

Other countries, including Great Britain and Sweden, have state churches. But the governments of these nations grant freedom of worship to other religious groups. In some countries, the government provides equal support for all religions.

Case Study on Martin Luther and the Jews: Religious Intolerance in the 16th Century

Introduction

Martin Luther is best known as the German, 16th century monk that broke away from the Catholic Church, began the Protestant movement, and founded the Lutheran Church. Luther was also a prolific writer. His translation of the Bible into German is considered a literary masterpiece. In addition to translating the Bible, Luther authored the *Small Catechism* (often referred to as the layman's Bible), hymns, and many theological writings.

The subject of this case study is a tract Luther wrote in 1543, "On the Jews and Their Lies." Readers will probably be surprised by Luther's severity and harsh words against the Jews. When the tract was first published, it shocked and dismayed many of Luther's Jewish and Protestant contemporaries.

For many years, scholars have tried to understand why Luther wrote "On the Jews and Their Lies." A variety of explanations have been offered: Luther's declining health in his later years; his frustration at the Jews' refusal to convert to Christianity; his fear of Jewish influence in interpretations of the Old Testament. However, it has also been suggested that Luther's attitude toward the Jews was the result of ingrained medieval prejudices.

Medieval Europe was dominated by Christian institutions that had produced a highly negative image of the Jew, particularly the Catholic Church. This period of history was one of constant Jewish persecution: key Protestant and Catholic leaders wrote condemnatory tracts against the Jews; the Jews were seen as the cause of all sorts of evil; and they were expelled from many countries throughout Europe.

Luther was prompted to write "On the Jews and their Lies" after a friend sent him a Jewish apologetic pamphlet and asked Luther to respond. After Luther wrote the tract, there was a particularly strong reaction from one member of the Jewish community. That was the voice of Rabbi Josel of Rosheim, a prominent, 16th century Jewish leader. Rabbi Josel had befriended several German leaders, including the Magistrate of Strasbourg. After the publication of Luther's tract, Rabbi Josel appealed to the Magistrate that a second edition of Luther's book not be printed, and the Magistrate agreed to not permit a new edition of the tract in his area of jurisdiction. Rabbi Josel was especially astonished that a scholar such as Luther would advocate extreme measures against the Jews.

Fortunately, most people did not heed Luther's advice on how to deal with the Jews. However, many people do believe that Luther's tract played a role in influencing the Third Reich of Nazi Germany.

This case study, comprised of three readings, is intended to present Luther's tract for scholarly analysis and discussion. Reading two is a condensed version of Luther's tract, "On the Jews and Their Lies." Reading three is a Lutheran statement and Reading four is a Jewish perspective: both readings analyze Luther's tract from their respective theological traditions.

2 RELIGIOUS INTOLERANCE THROUGHOUT HISTORY

ON THE JEWS AND THEIR LIES

Martin Luther

Martin Luther was born in Eisleben in Saxony on November 10, 1483. He was ordained a priest in 1507. In 1512, he received a doctor's degree in theology and was appointed a professor of theology at the University of Wittenberg. Luther led the Protestant Reformation in Europe from its beginning in 1517 until his death in 1546.

Points to Consider:

1. Why did Martin Luther advise Christians to avoid debating the Jews on matters of faith?
2. Summarize the Jews' "lies." Why did Martin Luther refer to them as "lies"?
3. What does Martin Luther propose in order to deal with the Jews?
4. Compare and contrast Martin Luther's proposal with the actions of Nazi Germany.

Martin Luther, "On the Jews and their Lies," in *The Christian in Society,* ed. Franklin Sherman (Philadelphia: Fortress Press, 1971). Reprinted with permission of Fortress Press.

What shall we Christians do with this rejected and condemned people, the Jews? Since they live among us, we dare not tolerate their conduct, now that we are aware of their lying and reviling and blaspheming.

I had made up my mind to write no more either about the Jews or against them.[1] But since I learned that these miserable and accursed people do not cease to lure to themselves even us, that is, the Christians, I have published this little book, so that I might be found among those who opposed such poisonous activities of the Jews and who warned the Christians to be on their guard against them. I would not have believed that a Christian could be duped by the Jews into taking their exile and wretchedness upon himself.[2] However, the devil is the god of the world, and wherever God's word is absent he has an easy task, not only with the weak but also with the strong. May God help us. Amen. . . .

Do not engage much in debate with Jews about the articles of our faith. From their youth they have been so nurtured with venom and rancor against our Lord that there is no hope until they reach the point where their misery finally makes them pliable and they are forced to confess that the Messiah has come, and that he is our Jesus. Until such a time it is much too early, yes, it is useless to argue with them about how God is triune, how he became man, and how Mary is the mother of God. No human reason nor any human heart will ever grant these things, much less the embittered, venomous, blind heart of the Jews. What God cannot reform with such cruel blows, we will be unable to change with words and works. Moses was unable to reform the Pharaoh by means of plagues, miracles, pleas, or threats; he had to let him drown in the sea. . . .

---

[1] Luther's chief earlier writings on the subject were his treatise of 1523, *That Jesus Christ Was Born a Jew* (*LW* 45, 199-229), and the open letter of 1538, *Against the Sabbatarians* (cf. above, pp. 57-98). He had promised at the conclusion of *Sabbatarians* to deal with the matter further, but apparently the resolve mentioned above intervened. Five years later, however, came the publication in quick succession of three treatises on the Jewish question: *On the Jews and Their Lies, Vom Schem Hamphoras* ("On the Ineffable Name"), and *The Last Words of David*. Cf. above, p. 65, n. 1.

[2] A reference to the conversions to Judaism of which Luther had received reports.

Illustration of Martin Luther by Ron Swanson.

There is one thing about which they [the Jews] boast and pride themselves beyond measure, and that is their descent from the foremost people on earth, from Abraham, Sarah, Isaac, Rebekah, Jacob, and from the twelve patriarchs, and thus from the holy people of Israel. St. Paul himself admits this when he says in Romans 9 [:5]: *Quorum patres*, that is, "To them belong the patriarchs, and of their race is the Christ," etc. And Christ himself declares in John 4 [:22], "Salvation is from the Jews." Therefore they boast of being the noblest, yes, the only noble people on earth. In comparison with them and in their eyes we Gentiles (Goyim) are not human; in fact we hardly deserve to be considered poor worms by them. For we are not of that high and noble blood, lineage, birth, and descent. This is their argument, and indeed I think it is the greatest and strongest reason for their pride and boasting. . . .

But to strut before God and boast about being so noble, so exalted, and so rich compared to other people—that is devilish arrogance, since every birth according to the flesh is condemned before him without exception in the aforementioned verse, if his covenant and word do not come to the rescue once again and create a new and different birth, quite different from the old, first birth. So if the Jews boast in their prayer before God and glory in the fact that they are the patriarchs' noble blood, lineage, and children, and that he should regard them and be gracious to them in view of this, while they condemn the Gentiles as ignoble and not of their blood, my dear man, what do you suppose such a prayer will achieve? This is what it will achieve: Even if the Jews were as holy as their fathers Abraham, Isaac, and Jacob themselves, yes, even if they were angels in heaven, on account of such a prayer they would have to be hurled into the abyss of hell. How much less will such prayers deliver them from their exile and return them to Jerusalem! . . .

This I wanted to say for the strengthening of our faith; for the Jews will not give up their pride and boasting about their nobility and lineage. Their hearts are hardened. Our people, however, must be on their guard against them, lest they be misled by this impenitent, accursed people who give God the lie and haughtily despise all the world. For the Jews would like to entice us Christians to their faith, and they do this wherever they can. If God is to become gracious also to them, the Jews, they must first of all banish such blasphemous prayers and songs, that boast so arrogantly about their lineage, from their synagogues, from their hearts, and from their lips, for such prayers ever increase and sharpen God's wrath toward them. However, they will not do this, nor will they humble themselves abjectly, except for a few individuals whom God draws unto himself particularly and delivers from their terrible ruin.

The other boast and nobility over which the Jews gloat and because of which they haughtily and vainly despise all mankind is their circumcision, which they received from Abraham. My God, what we Gentiles have to put up with in their synagogues, prayers, songs, and doctrines! What a stench we poor people are in their nostrils because we are not circumcised! Indeed, God himself must again submit to miserable torment—if I may put it thus—as they confront him with inexpressible presumption, and boast: "Praised be Thou, King of the world, who singled us out from all the nations and sanctified us by the covenant of circumcision!"[3] And similarly with many other words, the tenor of all of which is that God should esteem them above all the rest of the world because they in compliance with his decree are circumcised,

_____

[3] A paraphrase, rather than a direct quotation from Luther's source, *Der gantz Judisch glaub,* the section on circumcision.

and that he should condemn all other people, just as they do and wish to do.

Now just behold these miserable, blind, and senseless people. In the first place (as I said previously in regard to physical birth), if I were to concede that circumcision is sufficient to make them a people of God, or to sanctify and set them apart before God from all other nations, then the conclusion would have to be this: Whoever was circumcised could not be evil nor could he be damned. Nor would God permit this to happen, if he regarded circumcision as imbued with such holiness and power. Just as we Christians say: Whoever has faith cannot be evil and cannot be damned so long as faith endures. For God regards faith as so precious, valuable, and powerful that it will surely sanctify and prevent him who has faith and retains his faith from being lost or becoming evil. But I shall let this go for now.

In the second place, we note here again how the Jews provoke God's anger more and more with such prayer. For there they stand and defame God with a blasphemous, shameful, and impudent lie. They are so blind and stupid that they see neither the words found in Genesis 17 nor the whole of Scripture, which mightily and explicitly condemns this lie. For in Genesis 17 [:12 f.] Moses states that Abraham was ordered to circumcise not only his son Isaac—who at the time was not yet born—but all the males born in his house, whether sons or servants, including the slaves. All of these were circumcised on a day together with Abraham; Ishmael too, who at the time was thirteen years of age, as the text informs us. Thus the covenant or decree of circumcision encompasses the entire seed of all the descendants of Abraham, particularly Ishmael, who was the first seed of Abraham to be circumcised. Accordingly, Ishmael is not only the equal of his brother Isaac, but he might even—if this were to be esteemed before God—be entitled to boast of his circumcision more than Isaac, since he was circumcised one year sooner. In view of this, the Ishmaelites might well enjoy a higher repute than the Israelites, for their forefather Ishmael was circumcised before Isaac, the progenitor of the Israelites, was born.

Why then do the Jews lie so shamefully before God in their prayer and preaching, as though circumcision were theirs alone, through which they were set apart from all other nations and thus they alone are God's holy people? They should really (if they were capable of it) be a bit ashamed before the Ishmaelites, the Edomites, and other nations when they consider that they were at all times a small nation, scarcely a handful of people in comparison with others who were also Abraham's seed and were also circumcised, and who indubitably transmitted such a command of their father Abraham to their descendants; and that the circumcision transmitted to the one son Isaac is rather insignificant when compared with the circumcision transmitted to Abraham's other sons. For Scripture records that Ishmael, Abraham's son, became a great nation, that he begot twelve princes, also that the six sons of Keturah (Genesis 25 [:1 ff.]), possessed much greater areas of land than Israel.

19

And undoubtedly these observed the rite of circumcision handed down to them by their fathers. . . .

Therefore it is not a clever and ingenious, but a clumsy, foolish, and stupid lie when the Jews boast of their circumcision before God, presuming that God should regard them graciously for that reason, though they should certainly know from Scripture that they are not the only race circumcised in compliance with God's decree, and that they cannot on that account be God's special people. Something more, different, and greater is necessary for that, since the Ishmaelites, the Edomites, the Midianites, and other descendants of Abraham may equally comfort themselves with this glory, even before God himself. For with regard to birth and circumcision these are, as already said, their equals. . . .

In the third place, they are very conceited because God spoke with them and issued them the law of Moses on Mount Sinai. . . .

Learn from this, dear Christian, what you are doing if you permit the blind Jews to mislead you. Then the saying will truly apply, "When a blind man leads a blind man, both will fall into the pit" [cf. Luke 6:39]. You cannot learn anything from them except how to misunderstand the divine commandments, and, despite this, boast haughtily over against the Gentiles— who really are much better before God than they, since they do not have such pride of holiness and yet keep far more of the law than these arrogant saints and damned blasphemers and liars. . . .

In the fourth place,[4] they pride themselves tremendously on having received the land of Canaan, the city of Jerusalem, and the temple from God. . . .

The devil with all his angels has taken possession of this people, so that they always exalt external things—their gifts, their deeds, their works—before God, which is tantamount to offering God the empty shells without the kernels. These they expect God to esteem and by reason of them accept them as his people, and exalt and bless them above all Gentiles. But that he wants his laws observed and wants to be honored by them as God, this they do not want to consider. Thus the words of Moses are fulfilled when he says [Deut. 32:21] that God will not regard them as his people, since they do not regard him as their God. Hosea 2 [cf. 1:9] expresses the same thought. . . .

What shall we Christians do with this rejected and condemned people, the Jews? Since they live among us, we dare not tolerate their conduct, now that we are aware of their lying and reviling and blaspheming. If we do, we become sharers in their lies, cursing, and blasphemy. Thus we cannot extinguish the unquenchable fire of divine wrath, of

---

[4] The first three points have dealt with the Jews' claims resting on their lineage (above, pp. 140 ff.), on the covenant of circumcision (pp. 149 ff.), and on their possession of the law (pp. 164 ff.).

which the prophets speak, nor can we convert the Jews. With prayer and the fear of God we must practice a sharp mercy to see whether we might save at least a few from the glowing flames. We dare not avenge ourselves. Vengeance a thousand times worse than we could wish them already has them by the throat. I shall give you my sincere advice:[5]

First, to set fire to their synagogues or schools and to bury and cover with dirt whatever will not burn, so that no man will ever again see a stone or cinder of them. This is to be done in honor of our Lord and of Christendom, so that God might see that we are Christians, and do not condone or knowingly tolerate such public lying, cursing, and blaspheming of his Son and of his Christians. For whatever we tolerated in the past unknowingly—and I myself was unaware of it—will be pardoned by God. But if we, now that we are informed, were to protect and shield such a house for the Jews, existing right before our very nose, in which they lie about, blaspheme, curse, vilify, and defame Christ and us, it would be the same as if we were doing all this and even worse ourselves, as we very well know.

In Deuteronomy 13 [:12 ff.] Moses writes that any city that is given to idolatry shall be totally destroyed by fire, and nothing of it shall be preserved. If he were alive today, he would be the first to set fire to the synagogues and houses of the Jews. For in Deuteronomy 4 [:2] and 12 [:32] he commanded very explicitly that nothing is to be added to or subtracted from his law. And Samuel says in I Samuel 15 [:23] that disobedience to God is idolatry. Now the Jews' doctrine at present is nothing but the additions of the rabbis and the idolatry of disobedience, so that Moses has become entirely unknown among them, just as the

---

[5] Most of Luther's proposals are paralleled in the other anti-Jewish literature of the period, but the specific formulation which follows may be attributed to him. Fortunately, most of the authorities proved unwilling to carry out his recommendations, whether out of horror at their inhumanity or out of self-interest (since Jews played an important role in the economy).

It is impossible to publish Luther's treatise today, however, without noting how similar to his proposals were the actions of the National Socialist regime in Germany in the 1930s and 1940s. On the night of November 9-10, 1938, the so-called *Kristallnacht,* for example, 119 synagogues in all parts of Germany, together with many Jewish homes and shops, were burned to the ground (cf. William H. Shirer, *The Rise and Fall of the Third Reich: A History of Nazi Germany* [New York: Simon and Shuster, 1960), pp. 430 ff.].In subsequently undertaking the physical annihilation of the Jews, however, the Nazis surpassed even Luther's severity.

Bible became unknown under the papacy in our day. So also, for Moses' sake, their schools cannot be tolerated; they defame him just as much as they do us. It is not necessary that they have their own free churches for such idolatry.

Second, I advise that their houses also be razed and destroyed. For they pursue in them the same aims as in their synagogues. Instead they might be lodged under a roof or in a barn, like the gypsies. This will bring home to them the fact that they are not masters in our country, as they boast, but that they are living in exile and in captivity, as they incessantly wail and lament about us before God.

Third, I advise that all their prayer books and Talmudic writings, in which such idolatry, lies, cursing, and blasphemy are taught, be taken from them.

Fourth, I advise that their rabbis be forbidden to teach henceforth on pain of loss of life and limb. For they have justly forfeited the right to such an office by holding the poor Jews captive with the saying of Moses (Deuteronomy 17 [:10 ff.]) in which he commands them to obey their teachers on penalty of death, although Moses clearly adds: "what they teach you in accord with the law of the Lord." Those villains ignore that. They wantonly employ the poor people's obedience contrary to the law of the Lord and infuse them with this poison, cursing, and blasphemy. In the same way the pope also held us captive with the declaration in Matthew 16 [:18], "You are Peter," etc. inducing us to believe all the lies and deceptions that issued from his devilish mind. He did not teach in accord with the word of God, and therefore he forfeited the right to teach.

Fifth, I advise that safe-conduct on the highways be abolished completely for the Jews. For they have no business in the countryside, since they are not lords, officials, tradesman, or the like. Let them stay at home. I have heard it said that a rich Jew is now traveling across the country with twelve horses—his ambition is to become Kokhba—devouring princes, lords, lands, and people with his usury, so that the great lords view it with jealous eyes. If you great lords and princes will not forbid such usurers the highway legal, some day a troop may gather against them,[6] having learned from this booklet the true nature of the Jews and how one should deal with them and not protect their activities. For you, too, must not and cannot protect them unless you wish to become par-

---

[6] Apparently Luther anticipates that the political authorities will find his proposals too severe. He envisions and perhaps even sanctions action against the Jews by a *Reuterei,* probably meaning a band of robber barons. Prof. Jacob R. Marcus, in citing this passage, identified Luther's "rich Jew" with "the wealthy Michael," court-Jew or Joachim II of Brandenberg. Cf. Jacob R. Marcus, *The Jew in the Medieval World: A Source Book* (Cincinnati, Ohio: Sinai Press, 1938), p. 168.

ticipants in all their abominations in the sight of God. Consider carefully what good could come from this, and prevent it.

Sixth, I advise that usury be prohibited to them, and that all cash
and treasure of silver and gold be taken from them and put aside for
safekeeping. The reason for such a measure is that, as said above,
they have no other means of earning a livelihood than usury, and by
it they have stolen and robbed from us all they possess. Such money
should now be used in no other way than the following: Whenever a
Jew is sincerely converted, he should be handed one hundred, two
hundred, or three hundred florins, as personal circumstances may suggest. With this he could set himself up in some occupation for the support of his poor wife and children, and the maintenance of the old or
feeble. For such evil gains are cursed if they are not put to use with
God's blessing in a good and worthy cause. . . .

Seventh, I recommend putting a flail, an ax, a hoe, a spade, a distaff,
or a spindle into the hands of young, strong Jews and Jewesses and
letting them earn their bread in the sweat of their brow, as was imposed
on the children of Adam (Gen. 3 [:19]). For it is not fitting that they should
let us accursed Goyim toil in the sweat of our faces while they, the holy
people, idle away their time behind the stove, feasting and farting, and
on top of all, boasting blasphemously of their lordship over the Christians by means of our sweat. No, one should toss out these lazy rogues
by the seat of their pants. . . .

For, as we have heard, God's anger with them is so intense that gentle mercy will only tend to make them worse and worse, while sharp
mercy will reform them but little. Therefore, in any case, away with them!

RELIGIOUS INTOLERANCE THROUGHOUT HISTORY

LUTHER AND THE JEWS: A LUTHERAN STATEMENT

Eric W. Gritsch

The following reading was excerpted from a speech given by Eric W. Gritsch. Mr. Gritsch spoke before the Lutheran Council in the USA's 17th annual meeting in his capacity as professor of church history and director of the Institute for Luther Studies, Lutheran Theological Seminary at Gettysburg, Pennsylvania. He earned his master of sacred theology, master of arts and doctor of philosophy degrees from Yale Divinity School and Yale University. He is also the author and co-author of several books.

Points to Consider:

1. Describe Christian-Jewish relations during the 16th century.
2. Why was Luther eventually influenced by established anti-Jewish ideology?
3. Summarize the four major emphases that can be derived from interpretations of Luther's attitude to the Jews.
4. Examine what the author describes as the ''three essential aspects of Luther and his history.''

Eric W. Gritsch, ''Luther and the Jews: Toward a Judgment of History,'' in *Luther and the Jews* (Lutheran Council in the USA, 1983), pp. 3-9. From *Luther and the Jews,* copyright © 1983 Lutheran Council in the USA. Reprinted by permission of Augsburg Fortress.

Medieval and 16th-century Christian rejection of Jews was grounded in a theological anti-Judaism, rather than ethnic, indeed racist, anti-Semitism. So to call Luther the father of modern, or even German, anti-semitism is not really appropriate.

There is hardly a more painful topic in Luther research than Luther's attitude toward the Jews. Luther's bitterly scathing outbursts against the Jews have caused pain along the nerves of many a Luther scholar and church body. Lutheranism is particularly afflicted with the pain which links Luther with Hitler, Wittenberg and Auschwitz, and German Protestants with the most vicious anti-Semitism.

Yet Luther's convictions about the relationship between the Christian gospel and Israel need to be presented in their historical context. Otherwise the full weight of this evidence would be lost.

Christian and Jew in the 16th Century

Christian-Jewish relations in the 16th century were decisively affected by an enduring anti-Semitism which advocated the segregation of Jews from Christians. Popular medieval Christian propaganda blamed Jews for natural disasters, for the "Black Death" of the bubonic plague, and for almost everything else that went wrong in medieval culture and society.

In 1348, for example, German Jews were massacred by legal authorities as well as by lynch mobs in Frankfurt, Nuremberg, and Augsburg. Many Jews were expelled from German cities in the 1480s.

Spain, France, and England refused to tolerate Jewish settlements. The Spanish Inquisition of 1492 expelled a quarter million Jews, who moved along the Mediterranean coast to Italy, Greece, Turkey, Israel, and Persia. Many ended up in a large ghetto in Venice. Some Spanish Jews, known as Marranos, succumbed to sociopolitical pressures and officially converted to Christianity but continued to adhere to Judaism in secret.

The "wandering Jew" quickly became known as a usurer*—even though large Christian business corporations practiced a more vicious usury. "Usury" and "Jew" became synonyms, and usurious Christians were called "Christian Jews."

---

*Editor's note: *The American Heritage Dictionary of the English Language* defines a usurer as a person who lends money at an exorbitant or unlawful rate of interest.

25

The medieval church supported the segregationist policies of the nations within the Holy Roman Empire. The fourth Lateran Council of 1215 decreed that Jews were to be distinguished through a yellow patch sewn to their clothes. In Germany, Jews were required to wear special hats. Since Jews were known as "Christ killers," stories soon circulated of how they continued to kill Christ in the transubstantiated Host. . . .

In short, every stratum of 16th-century society considered Jews the diabolical enemies of Christianity and a cancer in society. As Bishop George of Speyer put it on April 4, 1519, when he ordered the total segregation of Jews from Christians in his diocese, "They are not human beings but dogs."

The Rise of Luther

In the face of such hatred, since Luther led a movement against Roman Catholicism's tyranny, many Jews viewed him as a friend. Some significant defenders of Judaism welcomed Luther as God's agent sent to destroy corrupt Rome before the end of the world.

The Spanish Rabbi Abraham ben Eleizer Halevi advocated the apocalyptic notion that the time had come when God called on the world to repent and return to the fold of his people, the Jews. Lutheran and humanist interests in the study of Hebrew and the impending schism in the Western church convinced Halevi that the Reformation was the God-sent event which would make Judaism the religion of the end.

Other spokesmen of Judaism, such as Rabbi Josel of Rosheim in Germany, did not follow such apocalyptic lines of interpretation. Josel, who had met Luther several times and communicated with other Protestant leaders, was respected by Emperor Charles V and had considerable influence on him. Though not always treated fairly, Josel won enough friends and influenced sufficient people in higher places to avoid the persecution of the small Jewish community in 16th-century

Eric Gritsch, addressing the topic of Luther and the Jews. From *Luther and the Jews,* copyright © 1983 Lutheran Council in the USA.

Germany. Only a few hundred Jews were in all of Germany, with the largest community of 78 settled in Frankfurt.

Luther viewed his life vocation as that of biblical scholar and was called "a professor of Old Testament." Of the 32 years spent on biblical studies, he devoted only three or four to the study of the New Testament. He was committed to the view maintained for centuries by Christian analysts that the Old Testament had only one meaning: a "prefiguration" (*figura*) and "foreshadowing" (*umbra*) of the New Testament, the authors of which are in the "faithful synagogue," as he put it in his first lectures on the Psalms in 1513-15. . . .

In these lectures the young Luther laid the analytical foundations for a Christological interpretation of the Old Testament. Following Augustine's differentiation between the "letter" and the "spirit" in the interpretation of the Bible, Luther assumed with Christian hindsight that

27

such passages as Psalm 77.1 ("I cry aloud to God") spoke of a spiritual bondage to sin, death, and evil in the world. The psalmist, therefore, already points to a spiritual Egypt, marked by the yoke of self-righteousness, from which the spiritual exodus of Moses liberated the ancient people of God. Psalms and Exodus point to a final liberation by the Messiah, Jesus Christ.

It took only one further step to argue, as Luther did in his lectures on Romans in 1515, that those Jews who linked spiritual liberation only to themselves, as the exclusive people of God were self-righteous. Indeed, God himself hardened their hearts so that they, like Pharaoh (Exodus 14.4), would not let the divine promise of salvation go to others. Consequently, when Luther interpreted Paul's declaration that "God shows no partiality" (Romans 2.11), he depicted Jews as the people who "wanted God to act in such a way that he would bestow the good on the Jews only, and the evil on the Gentiles only." He accused the Jews of an idolatrous partiality.

Like many other biblical scholars, Christian and Jewish, Luther viewed his time as the end time—an apocalyptic age filled with trials and tribulations. The storm and stress of the religious struggle with Rome only confirmed the notion that Christians would be beset in these last days by foes from within and without. The pope and the Turks were such foes, according to Luther. But like the first Christians, Luther expected Jews to turn to Christianity, just as Jewish apocalyptic notions expected the nations to assemble in the land of Israel.

In 1516 Luther sided with the humanist John Reuchlin, who in a famous controversy with a fanatic convert from Judaism had advocated the study of ancient Hebrew. The convert, John Pfefferkorn, had written crude, polemical tracts against the Jews. Luther's long-time opponent, the Catholic theologian and churchman John Eck, called Luther a "Jew father." Adherents to the old religion and to the status quo were convinced that Luther's Reformation was synonymous with love for Jews and that Luther and his followers were the reincarnation, as it were, of these ancient embodiments of hostility to Christianity.

At the Diet of Nuremberg in 1522 a rumor was circulated that Luther had denied that Jesus was born of a virgin, that he considered him merely the son of Joseph, and that Luther had become a "Judaizer."

Luther's response was quick and to the point. In the tract "That Jesus Christ was Born a Jew" published in 1523, he affirmed his commitment to the Christological interpretation of the Old Testament but defended the Jews who, like him, were being persecuted by the defenders of popish Christendom. The Jews, he contended, "are blood relatives of Christ" and "we are aliens and in-laws"; they "are actually nearer to Christ than we are"; and they should be treated kindly. Luther concluded that the Jews do need to be converted but "not by papal law but by the law of Christian love." This was the friendliest Luther ever got.

28

Unsuccessful Jewish Conversion

Luther's own attempts to convert Jews proved unsuccessful. In 1526 when three rabbis visited him and discussed issues of biblical interpretation, Luther accused them of abusing texts and escaping from their true meaning. The encounter ended without mutual hatred. But Luther believed rumors of Jewish plots and conspiracies against him and saw in them the confirmation of his conviction that Jewish hardened hearts were destined only to become harder. . . .

The old established anti-Jewish ideology easily won Luther over, due in large measure to his frustration over the issue of Jewish conversion. By 1537 Luther had concluded that the reconciliation between Israel and the Christian gospel was God's affair rather than the church's obligation. In an open letter in 1538 to his friend Count Wolfgang Schlick, source of rumors of Jewish plots against Luther, he vented his frustration: "Since fifteen hundred years of exile, of which there is no end in sight, nor can there be, do not humble the Jews or bring them to awareness, you may with good conscience despair of them. For it is impossible that God would leave his people without comfort and prophecy so long."

The rest is sad history. Luther did not stop attacking the Jews, even after he had concluded that one must despair over the question of Christian-Jewish relations. He had drawn the same conclusion about the papacy, and he continued to vent his angry frustration about it. In a 1545 tract he called the papacy "an institution of the devil."

As odd as it may seem in hindsight, Luther wanted to preserve the religious, cultural, and political uniformity of Christendom during the last days of the world before Christ's second coming. Consequently he supported laws which prescribed the death penalty for those who denied the dogma of the Trinity; who repeated Christian baptism, as Anabaptists did; or who revelled against authority, as was the case with the Saxon peasants. They were all seditious and deserved to be punished severely by the ancient laws of Christendom.

Luther could not conceive of a pluralistic society in which people would live together and still have differing faiths or even belong to non-Christian traditions. To Luther the papists were heretical, the radicals in his own camp were blasphemous and seditious, the Turks were a foreign military threat, and the Jews were a fifth column within established Christendom. All of them had to be opposed in one way or another.

The Infamous 1543 Tract

Toward the end of his life Luther became convinced that Jews must be totally segregated from Christians. This is the basic thrust of his infamous 1543 tract, "On the Jews and Their Lies." After using a major portion of the tract to repeat the old arguments in favor of a Christological interpretation of the Old Testament, Luther followed through with a proposal for segregating the Jews.

This proposal can be read as a prefiguration of Hitler's "final solution": synagogues and Jewish schools are to be eliminated; private Jewish homes are to be torn down in favor of communal, supervised settlements; Jewish literature is to be confiscated because it is blasphemous; Jewish migration is to be stopped; Jewish money is to be used for the support of converts; and Jews are to be put to manual labor.

"Gentle mercy will only tend to make them worse and worse," Luther advised, "while sharp mercy will reform them but little. Therefore, in any case, away with them!"

Many Christians and Jews expressed their deep shock over Luther's outbursts. Among them was his friend Philip Melanchthon. But Luther ignored them and, perhaps to spite them, published two more tracts, one "On the Shem Hamphoras [the name of the Lord exposed] and the Genealogy of Christ" and the other on "The Last Words of David."

In these tracts Luther disclosed how greatly he was influenced by the extremely successful anti-Jewish propaganda disseminated by Anthony Margaritha, a Jewish convert to Christianity. Margaritha's popular work, "The Whole Jewish Faith (Der ganze judische Glaube)," presented a collection of gross anti-Christian polemics he claimed to be of Jewish origin, most of which turned out to be false. The authorities of Augsburg finally expelled Margaritha after the Jewish community successfully proved that he was lying.

Nevertheless, the deed was done and Margaritha was praised by the Christian establishment in Germany and elsewhere. Luther had swallowed these anti-Christian polemics hook, line, and sinker—then struck back with equally slanderous anti-Jewish polemics based on Christological interpretations of the Old Testament. . . .

Four Major Emphases

In Protestant, Catholic, and Jewish interpretations of Luther's attitude to the Jews, four major emphases can be clearly discerned:

1. There is a basic difference between the young and the old Luther.

This interpretation, quite popular in regard to other aspects of Luther's life and thought, depicts him as a friend of the Jews until 1523, when he was accused by Catholic opponents as a "Judaizer." Until then Luther expected a rapproachement between Christians and Jews, hoping for their conversion. But when he heard of Jewish attempts to convert Christians and saw Jewish influences in his own camp, he advocated a radical program of segregation, thus joining the defenders of the status quo in the 16th century.

2. Luther's anti-Jewish stance was fueled by a radical, apocalyptic world view.

This interpretation, strongly advanced most recently by Heiko Obermann in his biography, "Luther: Mensch zwischen Gott und Satan (Man Between God and Satan)," pictures a Luther who sees himself as one of the last voices in the wilderness of the end time. His rediscovery of God's unconditional love in Christ was matched, so the interpretation goes, by a rediscovery of the biblical Satan who tempts believers to return to the power of self-righteousness through obedience to law, especially Jewish law. The Jews, therefore, were to Luther the principal embodiment of Satan's work at the end time.

3. In his latter days, Luther was too ill to be his true self.

This interpretation pictures Luther as the old priest-professor plagued by gallstones, kidney stones, depressions, severe headaches, angina pectoris, and various psychosomatic conditions. He was no longer capable, in contrast to healthier days, of making critical distinctions between fact and fiction when he read the charges leveled against Jews by fanatic Jewish converts. His final outbursts against Jews, as well as against the papacy, should be dismissed as the fulminations of a sick mind.

4. Luther's attitude never really changed.

He stuck to the view, already clearly advanced in the first lectures on Psalms in 1513, that the Jews were the people of God who had received God's promise of an eternal relationship with him. This promise was fulfilled in Jesus Christ, and restoration of the old relationship with God and redemption from the sin of self-righteousness depended totally on complete trust in Christ. Failure to convert the Jews, he concluded, must be the will of God. Therefore, Christians and Jews were to be totally separated, if need be by force.

This last interpretation is probably the most plausible. But careful distinctions must be made between the 16th century and our own time in defining the anti-Semitism of Luther.

Luther: Son of a Medieval Christendom

Medieval and 16th-century Christian rejection of Jews was grounded in a theological anti-Judaism, rather than ethnic, indeed racist, anti-Semitism. The latter is the result of anthropological and sociological speculations associated with non-religious attitudes toward nature and human nature in 18th-century Europe. Its history is grounded in theories about a mythic "Aryan" race. . . .

So to call Luther the father of modern, or even German, anti-Semitism is not really appropriate. When he feared religious pluralism and advocated cruel means to preserve cultural uniformity, be it in his opposition to rebellious peasants or to Jews who were unwilling to convert to Christianity, Luther was very much the son of a medieval Christendom. But this does not exonerate him from the charge that he was a 16th-century anti-Semite. He was.

The question is: Why did Luther not develop the same critical attitude toward rampant anti-Semitism that he did toward the rampant deformation of the church which in turn caused a radical deformation of society?

Any dialogue about this issue must take into consideration three essential aspects of Luther and his history.

First, neither Luther's life nor his work was dominated by the issue of anti-Semitism. As priest, professor and reformer, Luther consistently wrestled with the Old Testament, but he did not single out Christian attitudes toward Jews as the principal issue. To him the "gospel" was *the* issue—the cheering news that God's love for his people continued and was most clearly manifested in the man Jesus, thus linking Israel to Christendom as the one people of God who must live to proclaim the promise of God's unconditional covenant of love. . . .

Second, Luther's "final solution" for the Jews must be seen in the context of a fast-moving reform movement threatened by various forces from within and without. Moreover, such final solutions had been proposed earlier by others, such as the highly respected German Catholic jurist and humanist Ulrich Zasius in 1508.

But Zasius, Luther and others were agreed it must be done in a legal and orderly way. Luther opposed any and all mob action, in contradistinction to other reformers like Balthasar Hubmaier in Regensburg, who in 1519 incited a mob to expel the Jews. Thus Luther called upon legitimate government, be it in church or state, when he demanded that measures be taken against the Jews—a rare stance in a time rampant with violence and deliberate lawlessness. . . .

Third, Luther succumbed to the evil of anti-Semitism through a theological failure of nerve. He so desperately tried to communicate God's unconditional love for Israel, as well as for the people of God called "Christians," that he could not stop moving from the proclamation of divine mercy to conclusions about God's wrath. When faced with what he considered self-righteous Jewish stubbornness in the matter of conversion, Luther no longer let God be God. One can know the hidden God with regard to his plans for the Jews, he decided: God had rejected them and was in favor of their rejection in the world he created! . . .

Luther's attitude toward the Jews illustrates the fragility of faith in a world plagued by suffering, evil, and death. Despite pioneering insights into the universality of God's love, Luther turned the "good news" of this love into "bad news" for Jews and others whose hearts seemed to him so hardened.

32

Given Luther's own view of Israel and the Old Testament, there really is no need for any Christian mission to the Jews. They are and remain the people of God, even if they do not accept Jesus Christ as their Messiah. Why this is so only God knows. Christians should concentrate their missionary activities on those who do not yet belong to the people of God, and they should court them with a holistic witness in word and deed rather than with polemical argument and cultural legislation. The long history of Christian anti-Semitism calls for repentance, not triumphalist claims of spiritual superiority.

Luther may not be of much help to post-Hitler Christians on the "Via Dolorosa" toward better Christian-Jewish relations. But as long as anti-Semitism survives among Christians, Luther cannot take the lion's share of the blame. We honor him best when we search our own hearts and cleanse our own minds from at least those evils which prevent us from living in tolerant solidarity with others.

RELIGIOUS INTOLERANCE THROUGHOUT HISTORY

LUTHER AND THE JEWS: A JEWISH PERSPECTIVE

Marc H. Tanenbaum

The following reading was excerpted from a speech given by Marc H. Tanenbaum. Mr. Tanenbaum spoke before the Lutheran Council in the USA's 17th annual meeting in his capacity as founder and co-secretary of the Joint Vatican International Jewish Consultative Committee. He earned his bachelor's degree from Yeshiva University and a master's degree in Hebrew literature from the Jewish Theological Seminary of America. He has been described by Newsweek *as "the American Jewish community's foremost apostle to the Gentiles" and by* New York *magazine as "the foremost Jewish ecumenical leader in the world today."*

Points to Consider:

1. Describe the medieval attitude toward the Jews.
2. Compare and contrast Luther's early and later attitude toward the Jews.
3. How did Luther's treatise on the Jews influence Adolf Hitler?
4. Summarize the ways in which modern-day church leaders are confronting the past.

Marc H. Tanenbaum, "Luther and the Jews: From the Past, A Present Challenge," in *Luther and the Jews* (Lutheran Council in the USA, 1983), pp. 10-17. From *Luther and the Jews,* copyright © 1983 Lutheran Council in the USA. Reprinted by permission of Augsburg Fortress.

'Know, Christian,' wrote Luther, 'that next to the devil thou hast no enemy more cruel, more venomous and violent than a true Jew.' Hitler himself asserted that the later Luther—that is, the violently anti-Semitic Luther—was the genuine Luther.

When the U.S. Postal Service announced approval of a commemorative stamp honoring the 500th anniversary birth of Martin Luther, the respective responses of Lutherans and Jews disclosed what profoundly contrary places Luther holds in Lutheran and Jewish history and in contemporary perceptions. Lutherans tended to feel a sense of pride, an appropriateness, in the honor bestowed by that commemorative stamp. Jews reacted with either disbelief or outrage. . . .

Welcome as has been the progress in Lutheran-Jewish relations in the past four decades, no person of conscience can rest content with such efforts in the face of the magnitude of the religious and moral challenge that the anti-Jewish writings of Martin Luther continue to represent. But if we concentrate our entire attention on Luther's anti-Judaic polemic alone, we could be diverted from the far more fundamental spiritual and human threat. Put simply, that threat is the pervasive tradition of the demonologizing of Jews and Judaism that has existed in Christendom from the first century until our present age.

What have been the major features of that Christian tradition for Jews and Judaism? In what ways have Martin Luther's teachings been related to that 1500-year-old legacy he inherited? What was Luther's "contribution" to the anti-Judaic culture? What was its impact on the response of German Lutherans in the face of the Nazis' barbarous assault against the Jewish people? And finally, what can we learn from this soul-searching for our life together today? . . .

The Middle Ages and the Jew

The peculiarly intense and unremitting hatred directed against Jewry in Christendom—and only in Christendom—can be accounted for, according to Christian and Jewish scholars, by the wholly fantastic image of the Jews which gripped the imagination of the masses at the time of the first Crusade in 1095-99. The Crusade began and ended with a massacre.

"The men who took the cross, after receiving Communion, heartily devoted the [first] day to extermination of the Jews," wrote the historian and philosopher Lord Acton. They killed about 10,000 Jewish people.

When Godfrey of Bouillon, in the summer of 1099, succeeded after a heroic assault in capturing Jerusalem, he spent the first week slaughtering its inhabitants. The Jews were shut up in their synagogue, which was then set on fire. . . .

35

In the eyes of crusading people, Professor Norman Cohn of Britain's University of Essex writes in his landmark study, "The Pursuit of the Millenium: Revolutionary Messianism in Medieval and Reformation Europe and Its Bearing on Modern Totalitarian Movements," the smiting of the Muslims and the Jews was to be the first act in that final battle with the prince of evil himself. Above these desperate hordes as they moved about their work of massacre there loomed the figure of the Antichrist. As the infidels were allotted their roles in the eschatological drama, popular imagination transformed them into demons.

But if the Saracen* long retained in the popular imagination a certain demonic quality, the Jew was portrayed as an even more horrifying figure. Jews and Saracens were generally regarded as closely akin, if not identical. But since Jews had been scattered throughout Christian Europe, they came to occupy by far the larger part in popular demonology, and for much longer—with consequences, Cohn states, that have extended down the generations to include the massacre of millions of European Jews in the 20th century.

Based on his detailed historic and theological studies, Cohn asserts that "official Catholic teaching had prepared the way" for establishing

---

*Editor's note: *The American Heritage Dictionary of the English Language* defines Saracen as any Moslem, especially of the time of the Crusades.

Marc Tanenbaum, speaking before the Lutheran Council in the USA's 17th annual meeting. From *Luther and the Jews,* copyright © 1983 Lutheran Council in the USA.

the demonic image of the Jew which dominated the imagination of large parts of the Christian masses in the Middle Ages and beyond.

Malcolm Hay, a Roman Catholic historian, similarly declares: "The machinery of propaganda was entirely in the hands of the church officials. Preaching, chronicles, mystery plays, and even ecclesiastical ceremonies were the principal agencies available for the dissemination of hate. Preachers dwelt with a morbid and sometimes sadistic realism upon the sufferings of Christ, for which they blamed all Jews of the time and all their descendants. For many centuries the bishops of Beziers preached a series of sermons during Holy Week, urging their congregations to take vengeance on the Jews who lived in the district. Stoning them became a regular part of the Holy Week ceremonial.". . . .

Satan himself was commonly given Jewish features and was referred to as "the father of the Jews." The populace was convinced that in the synagogue Jews worshiped Satan in the form of a cat or a toad, invoking his aid in making black magic. Like their supposed master, Jews were thought of as demons of destruction whose one object was the ruin of Christians and Christendom.

Hatred of the Jews has often been attributed to their role as moneylenders and usurers. But the fantasy of the demonic Jew existed before the reality of the Jewish moneylender, which Christendom helped produce by refusing to allow Jews to engage in any gainful economic, civil, and military functions.

Luther's Place in Medieval Anti-Semitism

That demonology which had fixed the image of the Jew as Antichrist dominated the medieval world into which Martin Luther was born in 1483. As Joshua Trachtenburg says in his study, "The Devil and the Jews," to the medieval mind in which Luther was nurtured "the Jew was not human, not in the sense that the Christian was." He was the devil's creature, a demonic and diabolic beast "fighting the forces of truth and salvation with Satan's weapons. . . . And against such a foe, no well of hatred was too deep, no war of extermination effective enough, until the world was rid of the menace."

Given that reality, that Luther as an orthodox Christian, a former Augustinian monk, could have passed through a period of philo-Semitic sympathy for Jews is all the more remarkable. Earlier in 1510 during the controversy over the banning of Hebrew books that rocked Europe, young Martin Luther had sided with the great Christian Hebraist, John Reuchlin, uncle of Philip Melanchthon, over against the fanatic Dominican and former Jew, John Pfefferkorn.

Luther's treatise, "That Jesus Christ Was Born a Jew," was greeted in 1523 with enthusiasm by Jewish readers throughout Europe. In it he hoped that he might "entice some Jews to the Christian faith" and wrote the following: "For our fools, the popes, bishops, sophists, and monks—the crude asses' heads—have hitherto so treated the Jews that anyone who wished to be a good Christian would almost have to become a Jew. If I had been a Jew and had seen such dolts and blockheads govern and teach the Christian faith, I would sooner have become a hog than a Christian. . . .

"For they have dealt with the Jews as if they were dogs and not men. They were able to do nothing but curse them and take their goods. When they were baptized, no Christian teaching or life was demonstrated to them. Rather they were only subjected to papistry and monkery. When they saw that Judaism had such strong scriptural support and that Christianity was nothing but twaddle without any scrip-

38

tural support, how could they quiet their hearts and become true good Christians?''

Luther concluded the treatise with the following comments and recommendations:

"Therefore, I would request and advise that one deal gently with them and instruct them from Scripture. Then some of them may come along. Instead of this we are trying only to drive them by force, slandering them, accusing them of having Christian blood if they don't stink, and I know not what other foolishness. So long as we thus treat them like dogs, how can we expect to work any good among them? Again, when we forbid them to labor and do business and have any human fellowship with us, thereby forcing them into usury, how is that supposed to do them any good?

"If we really want to help them, we must be guided into our dealings with them not by papal law but by the law of Christian love. . . . If some of them should prove stiffnecked, what of it? After all, we ourselves are not all good Christians either."

To understand why Jewish leaders in Germany and elsewhere perceived this Luther as a thunderbolt of light illuminating their otherwise darkened medieval landscape is not difficult. In light of this essay and for other more fundamental reasons, both Christian and Jewish scholars have observed that the Protestant Reformation has had Judaic inclinations: the zeal of Christian scholars for the study and use of the Hebrew language, a revolt from the complex and arid system of Catholic scholasticism to the seeming simplicity of Jewish teaching and dogma, and the effort to recover for the Bible its former centrality in Christian life, to name a few.

The papist enemies of Luther lost no opportunity to brand him as a Jew and as a Jewish patron. His doctrines, especially with reference to his polemics against idolatrous images and the worship of relics, won for him the title of "semi-Judaeus" or "half Jew." In one instance he said of the Jews: "They are blood relations of our Lord; therefore, if it were proper to boast of flesh and blood, the Jews belong to Christ more then we. I beg, therefore, my dear papist, if you become tired of abusing me as a heretic, that you begin to revile me as a Jew."

By the 1530s the central issue for Luther was the proper interpretation of the Messianic passages in the Old Testament. Highly concerned about the impact of rabbinic analysis which denied Christological interpretations, Luther appropriated all of the Old Testament in the service of the New. He left us nothing.

The Jews, Luther asserts in his first lectures on the Psalms given during 1513-15, suffer continually under God's wrath and are paying the penalty for their rejection of Christ. They spend all their efforts in self-justification, but God will not hear their prayers. Neither kindness nor severity will improve them. They become constantly more stubborn and more vain. Moreover, they are the active enemies of Christ. They blaspheme and defame him, spreading their evil influence even into Christian hearts. As for Jewish efforts to interpret Scripture, these Luther asserts, are simply lies. They forsake the Word of God and follow the imaginations of their hearts. He concludes that to extend tolerance to those who hold such views would be quite wrong for Christians.

Luther's Impact on Modern Anti-Semitism

In his 1543 treatise, "On the Jews and Their Lies," Luther rails against the Jews for nearly 200 pages in his powerful, lusty style, with a torrential outpouring of passion and hatred that makes the diatribes of his predecessors seem languid. "Know, O adored Christ," he writes, "and make no mistake, that aside from the devil you have no enemy more venomous, more desperate, more bitter then a true Jew who truly seeks to be a Jew."

Luther concludes his treatise with a series of recommendations to secular authorities on how to deal with the Jews. The duty of the secular authorities was to implement his recommendation, he insisted, and the duty of ecclesiastical authorities was to warn and instruct their congregations about the Jews and their lies.

As has been noted by Lutheran theologian Mark Edwards, neither the vulgarity nor the violence of these remarks is unique, comparable to his attacks on papal opponents and Turks. What is unique is the relative helplessness of these particular targets of Luther's wrath. Catholics could take care of themselves and give as well as they got. The Jews were at the mercy of their Catholic or Evangelical rulers and could do precious little to protect themselves.

Although Luther's savage texts enjoyed only a limited circulation during his lifetime and the next few centuries, his protective authority was invoked by the Nazis when they came to power, and his anti-Semitic writings enjoyed a revival of popularity.

"A line of anti-Semitic descent from Martin Luther to Adolf Hitler is easy to draw," writes scholar Lucy Dawidowicz in her classic study, "The War Against the Jews, 1939-1945." "Both Luther and Hitler were obsessed by a demonologized universe inhabited by Jews. 'Know Christian,' wrote Luther, 'that next to the devil thou hast no enemy more cruel, more venomous and violent than a true Jew.' Hitler himself, in that early dialogue with Dietrich Eckhard, asserted that the later Luther—that is, the violently anti-Semitic Luther—was the genuine Luther."

Dawidowicz continues: "To be sure, the similarities of Luther's anti-Jewish exhortations with modern racial anti-Semitism and even with Hitler's racial policies are not merely coincidental. They all derive from a common historic tradition of Jew-hatred whose provenance can be traced back to Haman's advice to Ahasuerus. But modern German anti-Semitism had more recent roots than Luther and grew out of a different soil—not that German anti-Semitism was new. It drew part of its sustenance from Christian anti-Semitism, whose foundation had been laid by the Catholic Church and upon which Luther built. It was equally a product of German nationalism."

"Modern German anti-Semitism," Dawidowicz concludes, "was the bastard child of the union of Christian anti-Semitism with German nationalism." This union had corrosive effects on the conscience of millions of German Christians, leading the majority of the German nation into blind obedience to a murderous state.

Although the church could have influenced Hitler in the first months of 1933 while he "had still to feel his way with care," writes Richard Gutteridge in an essay on "German Protestantism and the Jews in the Third Reich," the "vast majority of the church leaders and the clergy serving under them was eager to enter into the new order and to make their positive contribution there. On Easter Day, to give an example, Protestant churchgoers throughout Bavaria were told from the pulpit that the new state was reintroducing government according to God's laws and that the glad and active cooperation of the church was advocated in the task of creating a genuine 'Volksgemeinschaft' in which the cause of the needy and oppressed would be promoted. There was a paucity of concern as to what would be the fate of the Jews and others who would be treated as outsiders. It was widely felt that if certain Jews found themselves at a disadvantage, it was fair readjustment of balance. It would be regrettable if there were cases of violent and cruel treatment, but after all, a revolution had taken place. Excesses were unavoidable, but things would surely settle down."

Gutteridge documents a number of protests from individual church leaders and then states: "The church as a whole kept silent. No bishop, church government, or synod spoke out in public at this time on behalf of the persecuted Jews. Hitler and his associates had good reason to be satisfied that the church would not make overmuch trouble."

Our Present Challenge

Forty years after the Nazi Holocaust many church leaders have begun to confront this past in all its awfulness and face its moral challenge. It is a positive and hopeful sign.

We might all take heart from the messages issued in recent months by major Lutheran bodies. The Lutheran World Federation's Fourth Consultation on the Church and the Jewish People called for a purging by Christians among themselves "of any hatred of the Jews and any sort of teaching of contempt for Judaism."

The consultation further stated, "In his later years (Luther) made certain vitriolic statements about the Jews that Lutheran churches today universally reject. We regret the way in which Luther wrote has been used for further anti-Semitism. This matter will be the subject of considerable attention. . . ." Among themes suggested for such discussions are: the Christian understanding of the validity of the Old Covenant and the implications of such understanding for the theology of mission, the question of mission-dialogue, the Torah and its relation to the New Testament, what Christians and Jews can do together in service to the world, the meaning of the Messiah for Jews and Christians, and the meaning of "Dikaiosune" (justice or righteousness) for Christians and Jews.

We might find especially moving these words from a statement issued by the Evangelical Church in Germany (EKD), a group of regional Lutheran, Reformed, and United churches in West Germany, on the occasion of the 50th anniversary of Adolph Hitler's assumption of power January 30, 1933:

"We. . .cannot simply dismiss our history and forget about it. Things which are repressed are bound sooner or later to reassert their power.

"Today we again repeat, unreservedly, the confession of guilt made immediately after the war by the members of the EKD council then in office: 'Through us endless suffering has been brought to many peoples and countries. We accuse ourselves for not witnessing more courageously, for not praying more faithfully, for not believing more joyously and for not loving more ardently.'

"To the older people in our midst we say: Please do not close your minds to the truth of what happened. To the younger generation we say: Do not stop facing up to this truth. You are not responsible for what happened then, but you are responsible for how these events affect our history. . . .

"To the politicians. . .we add a word of warning: Be mindful of your responsibility. Injustice and want, the burden of unemployment and an unjust peace settlement were the breeding ground in which the National Socialist Party thrived. The selfishness and disunity of the democratic parties brought Hitler to power. This is why it is essential to preserve social peace and also why the common commitment to a democratic, constitutional state must stand above all argument, however necessary.

"To all our fellow citizens we say: Do not allow yourselves to be persuaded again into a new hate. Hitler's rule was based on hate. This is why hatred must have no place among us, whether it be of external enemies, foreigners or other classes, groups, or minorities.

"Lastly, to our own parishes and congregations we say: Resist the heresy of believing in salvation of this world. Hitler's victory was also a victory for heresy. . . . In the words of our predecessors at the end of the war we too acknowledge that 'our hope is in the God of grace and mercy that he will use our churches as his instruments. . .to proclaim his Word and to make his will obeyed among ourselves and among our whole people.'"

Martin Luther was a deeply committed Christian seized by a vision of God trying to bring about salvation. In the process he manifested his many gifts as a man of no small achievement: translator of the Bible, even helping to establish the German language; writer of magnificent essays; fighter against the domination of the papacy and an arid scholasticism in a freeing of conscience with which Jews identified.

The task for us in this time, this age of pluralism and growing dialogue, is to try to approach the issue of Luther and his teachings with something of the same method by which many Christians and Jews today approach the cumbersomeness of their inherited tradition. Our task always is to separate out the essential teachings of the faith which are healing and redemptive, productive of love and mutual respect, and simply to reject that of the past which is no longer relevant or appropriate and was a historical response for another time. . . .

If there's anything that should characterize the observance of the 500th birthday of Luther, I feel it should be the determination to face the bad in past tradition and to replace it by building a culture filled with caring, understanding and—above all—knowledge of one another, not as caricatures and stereotypes, but as we are, committed Jews and Christians.

PART I
RECOGNIZING
AUTHOR'S POINT OF VIEW

This activity may be used as an individualized study guide for students in libraries and resource centers or as a discussion catalyst in small group and classroom discussions.

The capacity to recognize an author's point of view is an essential reading skill. Many readers do not make clear distinctions between descriptive articles that relate factual information and articles that express a point of view. Think about the readings in chapter one. Are these readings essentially descriptive articles that relate factual information or articles that attempt to persuade through editorial commentary and analysis?

Guidelines

1. The following are brief descriptions of sources that appeared in chapter one. Choose one of the following source descriptions that best defines each source in chapter one.

Source Descriptions

a. Essentially an article that relates factual information
b. Essentially an article that expresses editorial points of view
c. Both of the above
d. Neither of the above

Sources in Chapter One

__ Source One
"Religion and Politics: An Overview," by *World Book Encyclopedia*

44

— Source Two
"On the Jews and Their Lies," by Martin Luther

— Source Three
"Luther and the Jews: A Lutheran Statement," by Eric W. Gritsch

— Source Four
"Luther and the Jews: A Jewish Perspective," by Marc H. Tanenbaum

2. Summarize the author's point of view in one to three sentences for each of the readings in chapter one.

3. After careful consideration, pick out one reading that you think is the most reliable source. Be prepared to explain the reasons for your choice in a general class discussion.

PART II
EXAMINING COUNTERPOINTS

This activity may be used as an individualized study guide for students in libraries and resource centers or as a discussion catalyst in small group and classroom discussions.

The Point

It is difficult to understand the behavior of most German Protestants in the first Nazi years unless one is aware of two things: their history and the influence of Martin Luther.* The great founder of Protestantism was both a passionate anti-Semite and a ferocious believer in absolute obedience to political authority. He wanted Germany rid of the Jews and when they were sent away he advised that they be deprived of "All their cash and jewels and silver and gold" and, futhermore, "that their synagogues or schools be set on fire, that their houses be broken up and destroyed . . . and they be put under a roof or stable, like the gypsies . . . in misery and captivity as they incessantly lament and complain to God about us"—advice that was literally followed four centuries later by Hitler, Goering and Himmler.

In what was perhaps the only popular revolt in German history, the peasant uprising of 1525, Luther advised the princes to adopt the most ruthless measures against the "mad dogs," as he called the desperate, downtrodden peasants. Here, as in his utterances about the Jews, Luther employed a coarseness and brutality of language unequaled in German history until the Nazi time. [William L. Shirer, *The Rise and Fall of the Third Reich* (Greenwich, Conn.: Fawcett Publications, 1962), pp. 326-327.]

---

*To avoid any misunderstanding, it might be well to point out here that the author is a Protestant.

The Counterpoint

Paul Johnson's documentation of the holocaust and Hitler's racial policy is detailed and comprehensive. No mention whatever is made of any role of Martin Luther in the development of Hitler's policy. William Shirer, on the contrary, was content to promote his own unfounded and undocumented assumption that Martin Luther was at the root of Hitler's racism. . . .

If we are still troubled by the harshness of Luther's advice regarding the Jews, we must remember that we live under a system that has made provision for religious liberty and a plurality of religions. Luther did not.

It is gratifying to know, however, that among the reformers of the sixteenth century Luther was alone in disavowing any use of force in the proclamation of the gospel or in dealing with religious dissenters. Calvin sent Servetus to the stake for denying the Trinity. The Zwinglians drowned Anabaptist heretics. Tudor rulers in an enlightened England sent a thousand dissenters, both Catholic and Protestant, to their deaths. And all this is to say nothing of the Roman Catholic crusades, the French massacre of St. Bartholomew, and the Spanish Inquisition. [Neelak S. Tjernagel, *Martin Luther and the Jewish People* (Milwaukee: Northwestern Publishing House, 1985), pp. 85-86.]

Guidelines

Examine the counterpoints above and then consider the following questions:

1. Do you agree more with the point or counterpoint? Why?

2. Which reading in chapter one best illustrates the point?

3. Which reading best illustrates the counterpoint?

CHAPTER 2

CHURCH/STATE SEPARATION: THE PHILOSOPHICAL FOUNDATIONS

CHURCH/STATE
SEPARATION

RESISTING
RELIGIOUS INTOLERANCE

John Buchanan, Jr.

John Buchanan, Jr., presented the following testimony in his capacity as chairman of the board of People for the American Way, a nonprofit, nonpartisan, First Amendment citizens' group working to protect individual freedoms. He also served as congressman for the State of Alabama.

Points to Consider:

1. Define "morality." Define "religious doctrine." Which is an unacceptable basis for public policy and why?
2. Explain why some fundamentalist and evangelical church leaders are seeking exemption from basic American legal requirements.
3. Why should the government show neither official approval nor disapproval of religion?
4. Provide specific examples of religious intolerance.

Excerpted from testimony of John Buchanan, Jr., before the Senate Subcommittee on the Constitution of the Senate Committee on the Judiciary, June 26, 1984.

The Constitution provides that while government must be neutral toward religion, it must also accommodate it; and accommodation is a two-way street. The same principle that requires government to make a reasonable accommodation to religion as a part of society requires religion to make a reasonable accommodation of government.

The American system of religious pluralism is unique; it developed largely because people fled lands where the mix was improper—where religious dissent and diversity were not respected. But the same Founding Fathers who took such pains to preserve religious freedom also brought religious values to bear in shaping their new land. An analysis of U.S. history, constitutional law, and political practice suggests some clear guidelines for mixing religion and politics.

1. Religious Doctrine Alone is not an Acceptable Basis for Public Policy

While morality is a legitimate element of public debate, there is a crucial distinction between morality and doctrine. Morality is generic; Jews, Catholics, Baptists, Buddhists, and atheists can all agree that murder is a crime or debate the morality of foreign aid, for example, despite their religious differences. But a religious doctrine, on the other hand, is acceptable only to those who share a particular faith and is not open to reasonable debate.

The distinction is explained well by David Little, professor of religion and sociology at the University of Virginia. Describing the views of Roger Williams, the colonial Baptist known as the "father of American religious pluralism," Little discusses Williams' belief that "there existed an independent standard of public morality according to which governments might rightly be judged" and that "a commitment to religious pluralism must rest upon a shared belief that civil or public morality is determinable independent of religious beliefs." Little concludes that "In a pluralistic society, it is simply not appropriate in the public forum to give as a reason for a law or policy the fact that it is derived from the 'Word of God' or is 'dictated by the Bible.'". . .

2. It is Legitimate to Discuss the Moral Dimension of Public Issues

This should be obvious, but some critics of the Christian Right overreact and try to push discussions of morality out of the public debate altogether; they are joined by many so-called "realists" who want to dismiss morality as irrelevant in foreign affairs. But American political

50

debate would be unrecognizable without moral argument, just as it would be without organized religious involvement. Columnist George Will asserts that "American politics is currently afflicted by kinds of grim, moralizing groups that are coarse in their conceptions, vulgar in analysis, and intemperate in advocacy. But the desirable alternative to such groups is not less preoccupation with this sort of question, but better preoccupation. . . . Absent good moral argument, bad moral argument will have the field to itself."

The distinction between morality and doctrine makes it easy to see that while it may be arrogant to talk about forming a "Moral Majority," it is at least within the boundaries of pluralism, while talk of forming a "Christian Nation" is not. . . .

3. Discussion of Morality is Best Applied to the Common Good, not Private Action

This is a time-worn principle that has come under recent attack, but it makes good sense for several reasons. First, there is far less consensus on the morality of private action than on public issues; this is particularly true in the area of sexual morality. Second, government cannot successfully enforce private morality that doesn't have a public manifestation; efforts to do so generally end up weakening respect for law.

On the other hand, government can enforce civil rights law because private bias has a public side—public discrimination against minorities.

Overemphasis on private morality can obscure the responsibility of religion and morality in protecting the common good. New York Gov.

51

Mario Cuomo expressed this well in a speech at the Cathedral of St. John the Divine in New York City:

> To secure religious peace, the Constitution demanded tolerance. It said no group, not even a majority, has the right to force its religious views on any part of the community. It said that where matters of private morality are involved—belief or actions that don't impinge on other people or deprive them of their rights—the state has no right to intervene. . . . Yet, our Constitution isn't simply an invitation to selfishness, for in it is also embodied a central truth of the Judeo-Christian tradition; that is, a sense of the common good. It says, as the Gospel says, that freedom isn't license; that liberty creates responsibility. That if we have been given freedom, it is to encourage us to pursue that common good.

4. Government has a Right to Demand That Religious Institutions Comply With Reasonable Regulation and Social Policy

The Constitution provides that while government must be neutral toward religion, it must also accommodate it; and accommodation is a two-way street. The same principle that requires government to make a reasonable accommodation to religion as a part of society requires religion to make a reasonable accommodation of government. Many fundamentalists talk of the "sovereign church" and view government as evil; they hold that because they believe in the Bible, they are virtually exempt from civil laws, a self-serving position with no constitutional basis. While the Christian Right likes to compare itself to the civil rights leaders of the 1960s, its approach has more in common with the anarchy of the Yippies than with the civil disobedience of Martin Luther King.

A number of fundamentalist and evangelical church leaders are seeking exemption from some of the most basic American legal requirements:

- Fundamentalist groups, claiming "Spare the rod and spoil the child" have tried to weaken state and federal spouse and child abuse laws.

- Fundamentalists (as well as some mainline groups like the National Council of Churches) have supported Bob Jones University and other institutions that want to keep their tax-exempt status despite the fact they they discriminate on the basis of race. They argue that their racial policies are part of their religious belief.

- A number of fundamentalists and evangelicals support legislation proposed by Sen. Roger Jepsen (R-Iowa) and Rep. Mickey Edwards (R-Oklahoma) which would gut the Internal Revenue Service (IRS) of its power to audit churches. The IRS audits churches to insure they they are in fact churches and are paying the required tax on unrelated business income.

- Many Christian Right groups take the hard line position that Social Security payments are an unconstitutional tax. They are trying to win exemption from the new law making participation in the system mandatory for all nonprofit institutions.

The Supreme Court has consistently ruled that the government may place some restrictions on religious freedom if it has a "compelling interest." Recent rulings have upheld this approach on both tax and Social Security matters. The Court ruled in the *Bob Jones* case that the IRS may deny tax-exempt status to schools that discriminate on the basis of race, even when that discrimination is based in religious belief. Chief Justice Warren Burger said "Denial of tax benefits will inevitably have a significant impact on the operation of private religious schools, but will not prevent those schools from observing their religious tenets. The government has a fundamental, overriding interest in eradicating racial discrimination in education.... That government interest substantially outweighs whatever burden denial of tax benefits places on petitioners' exercise of their religious beliefs."

On Social Security, mainline religious groups overwhelmingly support mandatory coverage for nonprofit institutions; 85 percent of all nonprofits were already covered before the new law took effect. The mainline churches also view the issue as one that involves the churches' responsibility—to their employees and to the public at large.

Last year, the Supreme Court reviewed a case in which an Amish farmer sought an exemption from paying the employer share of Social Security because of his religion's belief that church members had a responsibility to care for their own people. The Court acknowledged the sincerity of the farmer's belief, but said it was overridden by the government's "compelling interest" in keeping the Social Security system intact. If the court won't exempt the Amish, with a venerable tradition of caring for their own people, there's no reason to expect it to exempt other churches.

5. Religious Institutions may Cooperate With Government in Programs Supporting the Common Good

The absolutist approach to church-state separation would bar this approach. For example, lawsuits have been filed seeking to ban as unconstitutional the use of federal funds for remedial reading and math programs for disadvantaged students in church-run schools. But as long as these services are provided regardless of the recipient's religion, there is no reason for churches not to participate. In one successful instance, a coalition of religious and secular voluntary agencies administered $90 million in emergency federal aid for the hungry and homeless in 1983.

Religious institutions, along with families, neighborhoods, and other forms of voluntary associations, are examples of mediating structures which help the individual cope with the larger institutions of society, such as big government and big business. These structures serve a variety of public purposes and may even be effective vehicles for delivering government-funded social services.

6. Government Institutions Must Show Neither Official Approval nor Disapproval of Religion

This is a restatement of the principle of government neutrality toward religion, applied to government corporate action. Justice Sandra Day O'Connor restated this principle well in a recent opinion:

The Establishment Clause prohibits government from making adherence to a religion in any way relevant to a person's standing in the political community. Government can run afoul of that prohibition in two principal ways. One is excessive entanglement with religious institutions....The second and more direct infringement is government endorsements or disapproval of religion. Endorsement sends a message to non-adherents that they are outsiders, not full members of the political community, and an accompanying message to adherents that they are insiders, favored members of the political community. Disapproval sends the opposite message.

7. There Can be no "Religious Test" for Public Office

Article VI, Section 3, of the Constitution declares that "no religious test shall ever be required as a qualification to any office or public trust under the United States."

But that requirement has come under attack in subtle and not so subtle ways in recent years....

The ban on religious tests is violated by groups like the National Christian Action Coalition and the Christian Voice when they label a candidate's position on issues as "Christian," "non-Christian" or "godless," especially on such issues as the creation of a separate Cabinet-level Department of Education or upgrading diplomatic relations with the People's Republic of China. Religious lobbies like Impact, Network, and Bread for the World have long managed to take positions and issue voting records without saying or implying that those with low scores are less "Christian" or less "religious.". . .

8. Once Inside the Political Arena, Everyone Must Play by the Same Rules

This means simply telling the truth, refraining from using scare or smear tactics, relying on persuasion rather than coercion and, in general, maintaining a sense of civility. It means, as Sen. Edward

54

Kennedy (D-Mass.) said at Jerry Falwell's Liberty Baptist College, that "people are not 'sexist' because they stand against abortion; they are not 'murderers' because they believe in free choice."

Cardinal Bernardin put it this way: "We should maintain and clearly articulate our religious convictions, but also maintain our civil courtesy. We should be vigorous in stating a case and attentive in hearing another's case; we should test everyone's logic, but not question his or her motives."

Another example of playing by the same rules is using a single standard to judge all participants in the process: for example, there's a double standard at work when liberals praise the Catholic bishops for entering the public debate on nuclear arms, but criticize them for entering the public debate on abortion. The bishops have a right to be in both debates; their arguments in each case are subject to the same level of scrutiny based on their merits.

9. Public Officials Have Every Right to Express Their Private Piety, and no Right at all to Use Their Office to Proselytize Others

While O'Connor's comment above was made within the context of direct government action, it also applies in principle to the rhetoric used by officeholders. To sum this up in the language of ecumenical dialogues, "Witness, Yes; Proselytization, No."

Americans expect, and even like, a certain amount of piety in their public officials, and national leaders frequently call for God's help in times of crisis. This is an expression of a non-denominational, non-threatening civil religion. Americans aren't threatened by a politician's private beliefs. . .

10. No One has the Right to Claim to Speak for God

The rhetoric of the Christian Right is full of references to America as a "chosen nation" or "the New Israel" and to "God's will." For example, Jerry Falwell has said, "God has called me to take action. I have a divine mandate to go right into the halls of Congress and fight for laws that will save America" and "Our battle is not with human beings, our battle is with Satan himself. The real conflict is between light and darkness, the kingdom of Satan and the Kingdom of the Lord Jesus Christ.". . .

The question of claiming to speak for God also comes up when religious leaders endorse political candidates. A minister has the same freedom as anyone else to endorse a candidate as an individual, but it's unacceptable to imply that an endorsement speaks for all Christians or reflects "God's will."

The Christian Right and its supporters argue that religion is an integral part of society and that both believers and religious institutions have certain rights. They do—but they also have responsibilities, including playing by the rules.

The First Amendment is the basis of so many of our liberties, that what begins as an assault upon religious freedom ends up as an assault upon all our freedoms. In recent years, political extremists have claimed a religious justification for censoring school textbooks, purging library bookshelves, and restricting students' rights to learn, teachers' rights to teach, and every citizen's right to speak freely. And that's only the beginning. In this century, we have learned of the horrors that can begin with book-burning and implicit attacks upon minority religion. Lurking behind the assaults upon the First Amendment is an attack upon the America we love—a melting pot; it is a rich mosaic of all the world's peoples, cultures, and faiths. From this diverse population is drawn the strength and hope of our country.

CHURCH/STATE
SEPARATION

RESISTING
GOVERNMENT INTOLERANCE

Dean M. Kelley

Dean M. Kelley wrote the following article in his capacity as the director of religious and civil liberty for the National Council of Churches in the United States. His article appeared in Liberty, *a First Amendment journal.*

Points to Consider:

1. Analyze the areas in which national or state governments have been intervening in religious activities or institutions.
2. When is government intervention legitimate?
3. Describe the difference between the Establishment Clause and the Free Exercise Clause of the First Amendment.
4. Summarize the government encroachment activities, as described by the author.

Dean M. Kelley, "Uncle Sam: Church Inspector," *Liberty,* May/June 1984, pp. 3-5. Reprinted with permission from Dean M. Kelley and *Liberty,* a magazine of religious freedom. Copyright 1984.

There is a growing notion that government has the duty to inspect, register, and certify religion as it does meat.

Too many civil libertarians are fighting a rearguard action against an enemy no longer present. Thirty and 40 years ago—and no longer—the danger seemed to be the overdominance of religious groups. And we went to war, not to the tune of the "Battle Hymn of the Republic," but chanting words from the First Amendment—"Congress shall make no law respecting an establishment of religion." For us, "separation of church and state" was a battle cry meaning "Stop the Catholic Church!" Or, for some, "Stop all the churches." Even today some libertarians seem more solicitous for the rights of anti-Semites, homosexuals, and pornographers than they are for the rights of religious bodies to live their chosen model of the good life as guaranteed by the Free Exercise Clause of the First Amendment. In fact, only now are we beginning to recognize that government intervention in religious affairs is the largest, most nebulous, pervasive, and portentous religious-freedom issue of our day.

February 1981 is a significant date in our growing awareness. On that date, groups representing more than 90 percent of organized religion met in Washington, D.C. The 280 delegates made the conference the most inclusive gathering of religious representatives in the nation's history! Why the meeting of such diverse bodies as the National Council of Churches, the U.S. Catholic Conference, the Synagogue Council of America, the National Association of Evangelicals, the Lutheran Council in the U.S.A., and the Southern Baptist Convention—all sponsors—and the Mormons, Salvation Army, Seventh-day Adventists, Christian Scientists, Unitarians, and a number of other unaffiliated bodies? Because of a common concern about government intervention in religious affairs.

Government Intolerance Issues

At the beginning of the conference the chairman, William P. Thompson, chief executive officer of the United Presbyterian Church, listed 17 areas in which national or state governments have been intervening in religious activities or institutions. Some interventions have been halted by the courts; others are still going on. Some may seem minor or even justifiable, but cumulatively they form an ominous pattern. Among the 17 issues were:

1. Regulation of religious fund-raising.

2. Lobbying disclosure requirements of religious bodies thought to be trying to influence legislation.

3. Regulation of curriculum content and teachers' qualifications in private religious schools.

4. Requirements that church-related colleges institute coeducational sports, hygiene instruction, and dormitory and off-campus residence facilities that they may consider morally objectionable.

5. Threats to such colleges and even theological seminaries to cut off loans or other aid to students if the schools do not report admissions and employment dates by race, sex, and religion, even though the schools receive no direct government aid.

6. Sampling surveys of churches by the Bureau of the Census, requiring voluminous reports, though the Bureau admitted it had no authority to do so.

7. Grand jury interrogation of church workers about internal affairs of churches.

8. Use by intelligence agencies of clergy or missionaries as informants.

9. Subpoenas of ecclesiastical records by parties in civil and criminal suits.

10. Placing a church in receivership because of complaints by dissident members of alleged financial mismanagement.

11. Withdrawal of tax exemption from various religious groups for alleged "violation of public policy."

12. Definition of what is "religion" or "religious" activity by courts or administrative agencies, contrary to the long-standing definition by churches.

13. Redefinition by courts of ecclesiastical polities, so that hierarchical churches are "congregationalized," while "connectional" churches are deemed hierarchical, contrary to their own self-definition.

14. Denying to church agencies or institutions the exemptions afforded to "churches," thus in effect dismembering the churches.

When Government Intervention Is Legitimate

The conference did not assume that government regulation or intervention is never necessary or justifiable; in fact, the concluding paper was entitled "When Is Governmental Intervention Legitimate?" The answer is, When necessary to protect public health and safety (narrowly defined, and not including such amorphous quantities as "public order, good, or morals").

The conference sought to correct the common notion that government knows best and can order the affairs of life better than individuals and private groups can if left to their own devices. Certainly religious groups over the centuries have done at least as well as governments in envisioning and embodying the good life. They invented and initiated general education long before there were public schools, and now the public authorities are trying to tell *them* how to *educate*? They pioneered in health care of the poor and aged long before there were public hospitals, and now the public authorities are trying to tell them how to care for people's health needs?—especially when the *public* institutions of education and health care often fail to live up to the very standards public authorities seek to impose on *private* agencies?

Private and church-related schools, hospitals, homes, and other institutions usually do as good a job as public institutions. Sometimes they do better, sometimes worse, but the very meaning of *better* and *worse* is precisely what government—except in the most obvious matters of health and safety—is not equipped to determine!

A good example is the Amish. Their mode and measure of education have been criticized by state departments of education as not preparing their children to survive and compete in the modern world. But that is exactly what they do not want to do, believing as they do that the modern, technological, materialistic culture is the very opposite of the good life! They want to live a simple agrarian communal life permeated by religious values, and it is for that they train their children. And they do a pretty good job of it.

The ideal education is one in which the younger generation learns by doing alongside the older generation, thus gaining the knowledge and skills necessary for successful living. Modern society has provided special environments with full-time teachers who try to impart a little of the "real" world into the classroom. But the Amish, who were teaching all their members to read and write back in the sixteenth century, when there was neither public nor private general education, already have the ideal educational arrangement of life apprenticeship in the "real" world. They educate successfully, with no felons or public dependents. And the public authorities want them to substitute artificial classrooms for the real-life experiences!

It is true that not many Amish youngsters become nuclear physicists—or want to, or know what that is. But they may be just as well off for that lack. It depends on what one believes the good life to be. And that is precisely the question that the government cannot decide, nor can all the citizenry voting en masse. Civil libertarians can get enthusiastic about the rights of *religious* alternative life-styles. The most untraditional alternative life-style going today is the Amish! Private school educators seem to aspire to shape their schools as much like conventional public schools as possible—all, that is, but the Amish, who want their educational process to be as much unlike the conventional model as possible.

Real civil libertarians, it seems to me, should be solicitous for the rights of religious bodies to live out their chosen model of the good life in maximum freedom. But the libertarian image still seems to be anti-religious and, specifically, anti-Catholic. Whatever justification there may have been for that concept and strategy 30 or 40 years ago, I submit that it is no longer justified.

The Roman Catholic Church today shows little of the aggressive, autocratic, triumphalist pretensions of a Cardinal Spellman (or when it does, they are soon deflated or disregarded by a very independent laity). The other churches are even less assertive in requiring serious discipleship (or when they do try to assert themselves, no one takes them very seriously, because they don't take themselves very seriously).

Much of the vigor and vitality in American religious life today is in the smaller, newer groups: The Pentecostals, charismatics, evangelicals, and the new religious movements often stigmatized as cults. They are the very ones of whom society is least tolerant—for the ironic reason that they are the ones for whom religion makes a real difference! If they were more placid and conventional in their beliefs and behavior they would get along a lot better—and make a lesser contribution to the health of the nation!

Ultimate Definitions

Vigorous and effective religion, I believe, is of great secular importance to society. The function of religion is to explain the meaning of life in ultimate terms to its adherents. If society does not contain within itself the means for such expression, it will be vulnerable to the maladies of meaninglessness that are increasingly prevalent today: disorientation, anxiety, resentment, bitterness, guilt, despair, vagabondage, various addictions, derangements, escapisms, and even some forms of crime and suicide. Because these may threaten the survival of society itself, it is of secular importance to society that thriving, effective religious organizations provide that function.

Governments have tried to ensure that function by "establishing" one or more churches to do the job. Unfortunately, the very act of establishing a religion tends to disqualify it for meeting the religious needs of those most needing help: the have-nots, the poor and oppressed of the population. After centuries of costly trial and error it was discovered that govenmental help to religion is no real help at all in getting the function of religion performed. So the founders of our nation tried a heroic experiment, and the only workable strategy for the public and the state with respect to religion: *to leave it alone.*

But now for 200 years we have been struggling with the fascinating riddle of what it means to leave religion alone. It means—among other things—that the government may not espouse, sponsor, promote, support, hinder, or inhibit any religion, all religions, or prefer one religion over another, nor may it become "excessively entangled" with religion. Thus the Establishment Clause has become well defined, but often at the expense of the second clause of the First Amendment: "or prohibiting the free exercise thereof."

Expansionist Government

The problem of the moment, as I see it, is no longer resisting the encroachment of expansionist churches, but resisting the encroachment of expansionist government. Too many militant civil libertarians are still fighting the battles of the 1950s, obsessed with the Establishment Clause to the neglect of the Free Exercise Clause. What is the difference?

1. Several federal circuit courts have studied whether public high school students can meet before or after class for religious study, discussion, or prayer on the same basis as other student groups do for nonreligious purposes. The U.S. Supreme Court has held that where a public university has created a "limited public forum" of this kind, religious interests cannot be disadvantaged because of the content of their speech. Two circuit courts have ruled that the same principle does not apply at the high school level, and the Supreme Court has declined to rule in these cases. A third case has now arisen in Pennsylvania, *Bender v. Williamsport,* and it will be interesting to see which clause of the First Amendment prevails. Will sponsorship by the school of extracurricular religious activities be seen as establishment of religion? Or will the court really focus on the religious liberty rights of the students?

2. Minnesota had enacted a law permitting parents who incur expenses for their children's education to deduct a limited amount of those expenses from their state income tax. This arrangement was challenged by the Minnesota Civil Liberties Union on the ground that it was an establishment of religion. But the federal district court, circuit court, and Supreme Court all found that it was not an establishment of religion, since it included expenses of public as well as private religion. No tax money was paid to parochial schools, and parents acted as a buffer

between the government and the schools benefiting from the tax deduction.

This decision, *Mueller v. Allen,* allows room for the free exercise of religion without significantly increasing the danger of establishment. Few, if any, parents are going to send their children to parochial school strictly because of the limited relief provided by this deductibility. It is also significant that the Supreme Court refused to base its decision upon the proportion of families benefited by the deduction. To send their children to parochial school was the parents' free choice and constitutionally should not turn on a head count of religious affiliations.

It seems to me that civil libertarians should encounter the danger of the movement—*government* encroachment—in this area as they have in others. They should take alarm at the growing notion that government has the duty to inspect, register, and certify religion as it does meat. They should be distressed that any citizens' group, but especially a religious one, should be expected, nay, *required,* to register with and report to public officials if they want a tax exemption, if they want to solicit contributions from the public, or if they want to influence legislation.

These absurd requirements, supposedly designed to prevent or expose fraud or manipulation, have produced elaborate bureaucracies that demand voluminous reports from private groups (thus distracting them from their own work) and that build elaborate files that nobody looks at. And all this they do without in the least inconveniencing groups that really engage in fraud or deception, because they can readily falsify their reports with little danger of detection, since bureaucrats normally view their function as compiling forms and filing them, not using them for any ultimate purpose. And there are already laws against fraud that can be used against those who are defrauding. So 99 percent of law-abiding groups are burdened with onerous and unnecessary and pernicious reportage without unduly deterring the one percent of miscreants the system was designed to catch!

I call it pernicious, above and beyond its bother and futility, because it encourages in the executive branch, the legislative, and even the judicial, as well as in the public at large, the notion that it is appropriate, prudent, even necessary, for the government to ride herd on these groups to prevent supposed dangers of fraud and sharp practice, which, of course, it doesn't.

Hanky-Panky: The Price We Pay

But what if government didn't do all this inspection and regulation? What unimaginable evils might befall? Think of the scandals of the Pallottine Fathers, the Cardinal Archbishop of Chicago, Jonestown, and all that! But a moment's reflection might remind us that, notorious as they were, and even if as bad as alleged to be, such scandals comprise a tiny fraction of total religious activities.

The Founders knew when they wrote the First Amendment that some hanky-panky might go on in the name of religion. That is the price of freedom. But they were willing to pay that price and take that risk. Are we less confident in the importance of freedom than they?

CHURCH/STATE
SEPARATION

SEPARATION OF
CHURCH AND STATE

People for the American Way

People for the American Way is a nonprofit, nonpartisan educational group founded in 1980 to promote and defend citizens' constitutional freedoms and traditional American values. The organization uses public education programs, citizen action, training, and the media to protect traditional American liberties.

Liberty & Justice for Some, *from which this reading is excerpted, employs a question-and-answer format to provide a quick, concise introduction to the issue of church-state separation.*

Points to Consider:

1. Define the doctrine of "separation of church and state." Provide examples of current church/state disputes.
2. How do ultra-fundamentalists interpret the doctrine of separation of church and state?
3. Did Jefferson, Madison, and the colonial statesmen write the Constitution as an expression of Christian values? Why or why not?
4. What do mainline churches and other religious bodies say about political activism?

David Bollier, Liberty & Justice for Some (Washington D.C.: People for the American Way *and* New York: Frederick Ungar Publishing Co., 1982). Reprinted with permission of People for the American Way.

The doctrine known as "separation of church and state" is a precious constitutional guarantee of religious freedom.

Q. The separation of church and state is just a creation of liberal courts. The framers of the Constitution never intended to prohibit government from helping religion.

A. The First Amendment is explicit in its intention, as are the historical documents written by Jefferson, Madison, *et al.* In order to assure religious freedom for everyone, the First Amendment specifies two limitations on government authority—the "Free Exercise Clause" and the "Establishment Clause." The passage reads: "Congress shall make no law respecting an establishment of religion, or prohibiting the free exercise thereof. . . ."

Because the doctrine of church/state separation restrains religious authoritarians in their effort to "Christianize" America, they must resort to some twisted explanations for why the "wall of separation" should fall. They blame "liberal courts" for misinterpreting the Constitution and dispute the meaning of tracts by the framers of the Constitution. They also portray the First Amendment as an oppressive restriction on their religious liberty. Televangelist Pat Robertson, for example, argues that Christians are in danger of becoming a government-persecuted minority, so a constitutional amendment "over and above the First Amendment" is needed. Such extreme action is necessary, says Robertson, because the "unelected tyrants" of the Supreme Court are making "a deliberate attempt to bring the United States into line with the constitution, not of the U.S., but of the U.S.S.R."[1]

This is a recurrent charge made by ultra-fundamentalists against church/state separation. They claim that just as the Soviet Union has purged religion from government and enthroned atheism, so too the United States is starting down the road to secular humanism and atheistic communism by prohibiting sectarian religious devotion from government activities. In addition, ultra-fundamentalists claim that church/state separation is a departure from the early history of our country. As the following pages demonstrate, this is patently untrue. But rather than admit the clear intention of the First Amendment, they blame scapegoats: liberals, atheists, mythical secular humanists, the courts, and so forth.

Q. What exactly is the doctrine of "separation of church and state," and why is it so important?

A. The doctrine known as "separation of church and state" is a precious constitutional guarantee of religious freedom. Without it, our government could try to prevent citizens from worshiping according to their consciences. The government could also force Americans, against their consciences, to provide financial and legal support to official state-sanctioned religions. Finally, legislatures could require that all candidates for public office meet certain religious criteria.

Over the years, the federal courts have developed three standards for judging whether a law violated the Establishment Clause. First, the Act must reflect a secular legislative purpose. Second, its primary effect cannot be to advance or inhibit religion. Third, the administration of the Act cannot foster excessive government entanglement with religion.

In addition to the "Establishment Clause" and "Free Exercise Clause" of the First Amendment, the Constitution in Article VI prohibits any compulsory religious test for public office: "No religious test shall ever be required as a qualification to any office or public trust in the United States." The principles for maintaining "a wall of separation between church and state" were included in this country's founding documents because they are considered basic rights of citizens, beyond the power of legislatures, presidents, or temporary political majorities to revoke.

Q. What are the most controversial church/state disputes right now?

A. The most enduring church/state controversies involve the government's authority to:

permit or require religious devotions in public schools;

provide tuition tax credits to private and parochial schools;

tax religious organizations;

require the teaching of creationism as science in public schools;

grant tax exemptions to private segregated schools.

But there are also a wide variety of relatively unexplored issues. How can religious broadcasters be regulated by the FCC without infringing on their right to the free exercise of their religion? May the government refer needy individuals to religious social welfare agencies? Is church missionary work violated by the CIA's use of ministers and missionaries? The breadth of church/state issues is more extensive than most Americans realize.[2]

Q. America was founded as a Christian nation. Our problems will continue to afflict us until we put the Bible back into politics.

A. The moral principles of the major religions have helped to build the character of our nation, but no religious creed has ever been officially enshrined as a constitutional principle. This is a core misunderstanding that motivates so many radical right campaigns: school prayer, creationism, and anti-feminism are all regarded as part of the crusade to "Christianize" America. The informal, ceremonial use of Christian beliefs, symbols, and rituals in American politics is a well-established tradition (as, for example, in presidential inaugurations, political campaigns, and the civil rights movement).[3] But this voluntary use of religion is different from government-sponsored laws that favor one religion or church body. Christian values may influence our lives and morality, but explicit sectarian religious doctrines may not be written into law. That represents an abuse of government power and an infringement of religious liberty. Religious liberty, if it is to have any meaning at all, must belong to all Americans and not just one group of Christians.

Q. Jefferson, Madison, and the colonial statesmen wrote the Constitution as an expression of Christian values.

A. Many ultra-fundamentalists argue that our political system represents the "Christian ideal of government" and that Jefferson, Hamilton, Madison, et al., were simply expressing their Christian values in writing the Constitution.[4] Although many of the colonial statesmen were in fact Christians, their political beliefs derived largely from "humanist" philosophers like Locke and Rousseau. It was Jefferson who coined the metaphor "a wall of separation between church and state" and who collaborated with Madison in opposing a proposed tax to support Christian churches in Virginia. Jefferson wrote in an 1801 letter to the Danbury (Conn.) Baptist Association:

> Believing with you that religion is a matter which lies solely between man and his God, that he owes account to none other for his faith or his worship, that the legislative powers of government reach actions only, and not opinions, I contemplate with sovereign reverence that act of the whole American people. . . building a wall of separation between Church & State.[5]

For his part, Madison was perhaps the most adamant defender of religious liberty. He played a major role in writing the First Amendment, enacting the Virginia statute for religious freedom, and drafting several of the Federalist Papers.

George Washington also resisted efforts to enshrine particular religions in the Constitution. One of his first official statements about church/state relations was made in a treaty signed with Tripoli in 1796:

> As the Government of the United States of America is not in any sense founded on the Christian Religion; as it has in itself no character of enmity against the laws, religion, or tranquility of Musselmen; and as the said States never have entered into any war or act of hostility against any Mehomitan nation, it is declared by the parties, that no pretext arising from religious opinions shall ever produce an interruption of the harmony existing between the two countries.[6]

It is perhaps also worth noting that in 1800, probably no more than 10 percent of the U.S. population belonged to churches, according to church historian Dr. Robert R. Handy. Another historian, Dr. William Warren Sweet, finds that "the great majority of Americans in the eighteenth century were outside any church, and there was an overwhelming indifference to religion.[7]

Q. But the First Amendment forbids only Congress from making any law "respecting an establishment of religion...." It says nothing about state legislatures.

A. Yes, but constitutional history and simple justice have made it applicable to all states. First, the notion of a *United States* is meaningless if one state is permitted to suspend rights intended for all Americans. Some states had established religions when the Constitution was adopted, but by 1833 all states had revoked official recognition to any organized religion.[8]

The Bill of Rights (and the Establishment Clause) did not formally apply to the states until 1868, when the 14th Amendment was added to the Constitution. The 14th Amendment states, "No state shall make or enforce any law which shall abridge the privileges or immunities of citizens of the United States, nor shall deprive any person of life, liberty or property without due process of law...." Although the 14th Amendment was meant to extend the religious liberty clause to the states, the Supreme Court did not formally decide this question until 1947 when it ruled in *Everson v. Board of Education* that the Establishment Clause does in fact apply to the states.[9] (The Free Exercise Clause had been applied to the states much earlier.) This ratified the principle that no state should be allowed to abridge the fundamental political rights guaranteed to all Americans.

Q. Christians have every right to be active in politics no matter what the First Amendment says about separation of church and state.

A. The Establishment Clause was never intended to exclude Christians or any religious group from political activity. Nor was it intended to insulate government policymaking from moral or religious principles. But the radical right deliberately misinterprets the separation of church and state doctrine as a ban on their political activism. Televangelists like James Robison use it as a convenient foil:

> I tire of hearing the doctrine of separation of church and state interpreted to mean that those who attend church or believe in God can have no influence in political activity or public policymaking. . . . I'm tired of hearing about radicals, perverts, liberals, leftists and Communists coming out of the closet. *It's time for God's people to come out of the closet and the churches to influence positive change in America.*[10] (original emphasis)

American public policy over the past two centuries has been deeply affected by religious groups. Some of these campaigns now seem quaint (such as the ban against dueling) while others are generally regarded as proud accomplishments (the civil rights movement and the abolition of slavery). Although some people may disagree with the policies that some religious groups advocate, religious activists cannot be faulted for exercising a "social witness" to their faith. In secular terms, it simply amounts to concerned citizenship. . . .

Q. What do mainline churches and other religious bodies say about political activism?

A. There is a general agreement among mainline Christian denominations in the U.S. that church bodies have every right to speak out and influence public affairs. This was explicitly addressed in the joint statement, "Christian Theological Observations on the Religious Right."[11] Among the points of agreement with ultra-fundamentalists:

> Christians ought to be actively engaged in politics and influenced in their political judgments by their faith in God and loyalty to God's cause;

> Church bodies and other groups of Christians have both the right and the responsibility to make their views known on public policy issues.

Senator Mark Hatfield of Oregon, who is both a practicing politician and evangelical leader, offers a similar viewpoint: "The Church can never make a true peace with the State and still preserve the wholeness of The Gospel by promising to leave politics alone and speak only about faith. Proclaiming the whole Gospel of Jesus Christ as Lord has inherent political consequences, as the early church quickly discovered."[12]

In an essay, "Religious Responsibility in a Free Society," the late Rabbi Morris Adler of Detroit made a similar observation: "Religion has no technical competence in the fields of politics, economy, and social need. But it does possess the qualities without which no adequate solution of the problem in these areas of our national life can ever be achieved, namely, large humane goals and a passion for justice and righteousness."[13] Needless to say, the spectrum of theological opinion on *what* constitutes humane and just policies is great.

Mainline religious groups acknowledge the legitimacy of secular political authority and accept the consequences of violating its laws. The more zealous ultra-fundamentalists, however, deny the legitimacy of *any* secular political authority. Televangelist Pat Robertson, for example, considers church/state separation a totalitarian doctrine:

"The government has come to think that really the church exists at the leisure of the government. In other words, the Supreme Court says churches exist because of a benevolent neutrality. That's a totalitarian statement."[14] Many in the radical religious right cannot understand that a benevolent neutrality is precisely what guarantees religious freedom for Americans with vastly differing religious faiths.

Not surprisingly, the moderate Christian denominations are dismayed at the selective and self-serving interpretations of the Bible that ultra-fundamentalists make. In their October 1980 statement, the 15 major church bodies quote theologian Reinhold Niebuhr: "The sad experiences of Christian history show how human pride and spiritual arrogance rise to new heights precisely at the point where the claims of sanctity are made without due qualification."[15]

Republican Senator Robert Packwood shares the consternation of his mainline church colleagues: "God did not speak to any of us and say, 'You are right and those who disagree with you are wrong.' If any of us thinks God has ordained us to speak for Him, we are wrong. Worse, if we are in positions of power and believe we speak for God, we become dangerous."[16]

---

[1] Editorial "Taking a 'Club' to the First Amendment," *Church & State*, November 1981, p. 195.

[2] See John M. Swomley, Jr., "The Decade Ahead in Church-State Issues," *The Christian Century*, February 25, 1981, p. 199.

[3] See, e.g., Robert N. Bellah and Phillip E. Hammond, *Varieties of Civil Religion* (San Francisco, California: Harper and Row, 1980).

[4] See, e.g., Rus Walton, *One Nation Under God* (Washington, D.C.: Third Century Publishers, 1975) and Peter Marshall and David Manuel, *The Light and the Glory,* (Old Tappan, N.J.: Fleming H. Revell Co., 1977).

[5] H. A. Washington, editor, *The Writings of Thomas Jefferson* (U.S. Congress, 1854) Vol. 8, p. 113.

[6] Treaty with Tripoli, 1796, Article XI, in Hunter Miller, *Treaties and Other International Acts of the United States of America* (U.S. Government Printing Office, 1931), p. 365.

[7] Robert T. Handy, *History of the Churches in U.S. and Canada* (New York: Oxford University Press, 1977). Also, William W. Sweet, *Revivalism in America* (Magnolia, Massachusetts: Peter Smith, 1944).

See also: Ashley Montagu and Edward Darling, *The Ignorance of Certainty,* "The United States is a Christian Nation?" (New York: Harper and Row, 1980). Also, Franklin Hamlin Littell, *From State Church to Pluralism: A Protestant Interpretation of Religion in American History* (New York: Macmillan Co., 1971).

[8] John M. Swomley, Jr., "Has the Supreme Court Eroded the First Amendment?" *Church & State,* December 1981, p. 252.

[9] *Everson v. Board of Education,* 370 U.S. 1 (1947).

[10] James Robison, "Commit to: Bible Principles—Not Political Promises," *Life's Answer,* October 1980, p. 2.

[11] "Christian Theological Observations on the Religious Right," statement issued by 15 major church bodies in Washington, D.C., October 20, 1980. Groups signing include: United Methodist Church, Lutheran Council in the U.S.A.; American Baptist Churches in the U.S.A.; Evangelical Covenant Church in America; Moravian Church, Northern Province; Christian Methodist Episcopal Church; Progressive National Baptist Convention, Inc.; Friends General Conference; Church of the Brethran; United Church of Christ; Baptist Joint Committee on Public Affairs; Christian Church (Disciples of Christ); Presbyterian Church in the U.S.; and United Presbyterian Church in the U.S.A.

[12] Mark Hatfield, *Between a Rock and a Hard Place* (Waco, Texas: Word Books, 1977).

[13] Morris Adler, "Religious Responsibility in a Free Society," excerpted from *May I Have a Word With You?* (Crown Publishers, 1967), in *Face to Face, An Interreligious Bulletin* (Anti-Defamation League of B'nai B'rith), Vol. VIII, Winter 1981.

[14] Rev. Pat Robertson, "700 Club" special broadcast, "Seven Days Ablaze", October 1981.

[15] "Christian Theological Observations. . ." op. cit.

[16] Robert Packwood, *Watch on the Right* (Des Moines, Iowa, newsletter), June 1981. Also, *Portland Oregonian,* August 19, 1981.

CHURCH/STATE
SEPARATION

THE CHURCH AND STATE
ARE NOT SEPARATE

D. James Kennedy

*D. James Kennedy presented the following testimony in his capacity
as senior minister of the Coral Ridge Presbyterian Church in Fort
Lauderdale, Florida; president of the Coalition for Religious Liberty;
and president of Evangelism Explosion International.*

Points to Consider:

1. Does the First Amendment teach separation of church and state?
   Provide evidence to support your answer.
2. Explain what the author means when he says "you cannot legislate
   anything but morality."
3. Define the secular humanist morality.
4. Why does the author equate the separation of church and state with
   Communism?

Excerpted from testimony of D. James Kennedy before the Senate Subcommittee on the Constitution of the Senate Committee on the Judiciary,
June 26, 1984.

The founders of this nation never intended for this to be a nation which was neutral toward God.

There are today several ominous movements going on in America and in the Western world, for the most part undetected by Christians, which I think portend great evil for the church unless we understand them and do something about them. There is, first of all, a tremendous change that is coming about in the relationship of the church and the state in America. It is happening so slowly that we are like that frog sitting in the pot of warm water which is gradually being heated to the boiling point. The frog just sits there and is slowly boiled to death. Like the frog, we do not even perceive what is happening! We have today, dominant in this country and accepted by 99 percent of the people, a view of the relationship of church and state which is almost diametrically opposite to that which was taught by the Founding Fathers of this country and which was expressed in the First Amendment of our Constitution. Yet, how many people are aware of that? If it goes unchecked much further it will, as it is beginning to do right now, bring about the destruction of the liberties of Christians in this land!

The First Amendment

Does the First Amendment teach the separation of church and state? I venture to say that 95 percent of the people in America today have been brainwashed into the place where they would say 'yes.' But it does not! I think it is vital that we understand what the First Amendment to the Constitution says, because the relationship between these two 'kingdoms' has been a long and difficult one. The Founding Fathers of this country, I think, resolved that question in a marvelous way but it is being completely destroyed in our time—and most people are not even aware of it. The First Amendment states: "Congress shall make no law respecting an establishment of religion or prohibiting the free exercise thereof." Question: What does that say about what the church can or cannot do? What does that say about what a Christian citizen should or should not do? What? Absolutely nothing! It says, "*Congress shall make no law respecting an establishment of religion or prohibiting the free exercise thereof.*" It says nothing about the church! The First Amendment teaches *the separation of the state from the church.* Well, where did we get this idea of a 'wall of separation between church and state'? That does not come out of the First Amendment. That comes from a private letter written by Thomas Jefferson in 1802 to the Danbury Baptists in Connecticut. He said, there should be "a wall of separation between church and state." Now, what is the difference between that and the First Amendment?

Our religious liberties depend on a proper perception of the difference between those two things. The First Amendment is a *one-way street.*

It restrains the federal government. The Bill of Rights was written to restrain the federal government from interfering with the liberties of the people, because they were afraid that the people of this new country would not accept the new Constitution unless the rights of the people were further defined and protected. "A wall of separation," on the other hand, is most emphatically a *two-way street.* It prohibits and restrains those on one side of the wall equally as much as it restrains those on the other side of the wall. Now we have a two-way street. But in the last several decades what has been happening? It has been turned around until now we again have virtually a one-way street moving *in the opposite direction,* so that 98 percent of the time in the last year (ask yourself if this is not true) when you heard the phrase 'separation of church and state' what was being discussed was: What the *church shall or shall not do.* That's 180 degrees off from the First Amendment of the Constitution! Now the federal government is unshackling itself from the First Amendment, and the shackles are being put on the church! . . .

Legislating Morality

Another ominous tendency is seen in the silent legal revolution going on in the Western world today. How many times have you heard it said that you can't legislate morality? Hitler was right! You can tell the big lie so often and so loud that people will come to believe it! "You can't legislate morality!" Like the separation of church and state, I am sure that the vast majority of Americans would say to that statement, "Of course you can't!" But I would simply like to ask this question, my friend: "If you can't legislate morality, pray tell me what can you legislate?" Immorality? The fact is that you cannot legislate anything but morality! We have laws against murder because it is immoral to murder; we have laws against stealing because it is immoral to steal; we have laws against rape because it is immoral to rape. This country's legislative enactments were founded incontrovertibly upon the Judeo-Christian ethic of the Founding Fathers of this country. Even Thomas Jefferson, who certainly was the least evangelical of the

76

founders of this country, said in his Charter for the University of Virginia, that the proofs for God as the sovereign Lord and Creator and Ruler of this world and of the moral requirements and obligations which flow from that, must be taught to all students. The legislation of this country was based upon Christian morality as revealed in the Word of God. This is where we derived our morality.

Secular Humanism

However, for the last four decades we have seen in this nation that the Christian morality is slowly being replaced by the secular humanist morality as the foundation for legislative enactments. When that substitution is complete you will find yourself living in an America very alien from anything that you have known. When all of their so-called ethical agenda has successfully been transformed into legislation this will be a different country than ever it was before. Such things as abortion (and you might consider the degree of success which they have already had), infanticide, homosexuality, free divorce, euthanasia, gambling, pornography, and suicide are simply a portion of the ethical agenda of the secular humanist, along with the total complete removal of every single public vestige of Christian faith and religion and belief in God that has made this country great. That is their agenda and they are eagerly and determinately and assiduously engaged in enacting it as the foundation of this country's legislation under the false teaching that the government of the United States is supposed to be neutral concerning God. They are taking the concept that we are not to have an established Church and moving from that to the concept that the government is neutral concerning God.

That is a concept which is worse than heathenism because even heathenism is based upon the belief in some diety! All government is based upon some religious or anti-religious system. What that means for us today, I think, is a very serious matter. This nation was never meant to be neutral toward God. James Madison, who wrote the Constitution, said that we cannot govern without God and the Ten Commandments. Now the Supreme Court, in its great wisdom, has said that the Ten Commandments cannot be put up on the walls of the schools of Kentucky—yet they are carved on the walls of the Supreme Court building! And the man who wrote the Constitution that they are interpreting, said that we cannot govern without them!

George Washington said it would be impossible to govern without God and the Bible. The founders of this nation never intended for this to be a nation which was neutral toward God. They did not hesitate to call upon God. They did not hesitate to mention God in their public utterances and in public buildings. They did not hesitate at all to make mention of Him or offer thanksgiving to Him for His goodness and providence; or to set aside special days of praise and prayer and thanksgiving to God, or establish chaplaincies for the Senate and House of Representatives and the Armed Services.

Separation of Church and State?

Now we are moving irresistibly toward the Soviet-Communist concept of separation of church and state, and that is very, very dangerous. The Soviets pride themselves on the fact that they believe in the separation of church and state, and America is moving rapidly to adopt their view. What is their view? It is simply this: the church is free to do anything that the government is not engaged in—and the government is engaged in almost everything! Therefore, the church is free to stay within its four walls, pray, and sing hymns, and if it does anything else it is in big trouble.

That is what is happening in America and, unfortunately, many churches and pastors and Christians are accepting it and even defending it!! It is the same sort of defeatist approach that we have taken toward the containment of Communism for the last forty years; that is, we have adopted the Communist view of our government toward religion. Remember what they said? The Communists said that what's mine is mine and what's yours is negotiable. And now that is what the government is saying! They are saying, What is ours is ours and it is political; therefore, it is out of bounds for you. And what is yours is negotiable because what is religious today and spiritual today may be political tomorrow when we rule it to be legal. For example: abortion, homosexuality, suicide, or anything else. When that happens, it is like the churches in California who were asked to sign statements, such as: Have you made any statements in the past year concerning such *political* matters as abortion, homosexuality, etc. What's mine is mine and what's yours is negotiable and we're going to negotiate you right into a little tiny closet! American Christians are sitting around just letting it happen, like the proverbial frog. And do you know why? Because we're afraid—we're afraid of the flak; we're afraid of the controversy. We've run and we've hid under our beds. We've forgotten the words of Scripture: "Fear not." Gentlemen, if you are going to be leaders, one thing that is called for is courage. I want to tell you, the secular humanists have declared war on Christianity in this country and at the moment they are winning the war.

Humanism is a religion. This is declared nine times in the Humanist Manifesto of 1933, and in the second Humanist Manifesto in 1973. It is declared repeatedly that it is a religion. The dictionary declares it to be a religion. The secular humanists declare it to be a religion. The Supreme Court in *Torcaso v. Watkins* has declared that secular humanism is one of the several non-theistic religions operating in this country. You don't have to believe in God to have a religion. Buddhism is non-theistic, as is Taoism, as is ethical culturism—these are some non-theistic religions, according to the Supreme Court. Yet secular

78

humanism with its tenets of atheism, evolution, amorality, socialism, and one world government, is taught in virtually all the public schools of this country. Therefore, secular humanism has become an established religion in this country over the last several decades, primarily through the work of such men as John Dewey and other signers of the secular Humanist Manifesto. It has become the established religion of America. Last year $31 billion plus was spent by the federal government on our public educational system with its establishment of the religion of secular humanism. The Supreme Court has declared that our schools cannot teach any religion, yet the same Supreme Court has declared that secular humanism is a religion!

CHURCH/STATE
SEPARATION

THE CHURCH AND STATE
SHOULD NOT USURP EACH OTHER

Charles V. Bergstrom

The Reverend Charles V. Bergstrom presented the following testimony in his capacity as executive director of the Office of Governmental Affairs for the Lutheran Council in the U.S.A. The Office of Governmental Affairs is comprised of three Lutheran church bodies: the American Lutheran Church, the Lutheran Church in America, and the Association of Evangelical Lutheran Churches.

Points to Consider:

1. Compare and contrast the terms "institutional separation" and "functional interaction."
2. Define "integrated auxiliaries." What role do they play in church-state relations?
3. How is the government trying to limit the church's ministry of advocacy?
4. Why do Lutherans believe prayer in public schools is not necessary and potentially harmful?

Excerpted from testimony of Charles V. Bergstrom before the Senate Subcommittee on the Constitution of the Senate Committee on the Judiciary, June 26, 1984.

Churches should not be in the business of using the coercive power of the state to enforce their versions of what is moral; similarly, the state should not assume the functions of the church in preaching or evangelizing, or determine for the church what is or is not part of its mission.

Many in this nation ground their understanding of the proper relationship between church and state on a somewhat simplistic interpretation of Thomas Jefferson's description of the "wall of separation" between the two institutions; they maintain that this "wall" creates a somewhat static situation in which church and state hygienically operate in their own spheres, never fundamentally affecting or "infecting" each other. But such an understanding of the "wall" does not do justice to the dynamic and continually changing relationship between the two institutions in this country. To echo Chief Justice Burger's 1971 observation, the "wall" is, in practice, more like a "blurred, indistinct and variable barrier."

The Lutheran churches I represent have described their understanding of the proper relationship between church and government in terms of "institutional separation and functional interaction." Thus, the "wall" of institutional separation stands within a grey "zone" of interaction between the two institutions.

Institutional Separation

We believe that both government and church have a God-given role in the world. The government is to establish justice, advance human rights, promote peace, and work for the welfare of all in society; the church's mission includes proclaiming the Gospel through preaching, teaching, administration of the sacraments, social service and advocacy on behalf of all members of the social order. Recognizing the distinctive role of each, we believe that they should be separate institutionally, and that one should not usurp the role of the other. Churches should not be in the business of using the coercive power of the state to enforce their versions of what is moral; similarly, the state should not assume the functions of the church in preaching or evangelizing, or determine for the church what is or is not part of its mission.

Even when each is fulfilling its legitimate role, there is a sometimes uneasy balance between the government's responsibility to regulate for the common good and the church's right to free exercise of religion. Generally, Lutheran churches maintain that the government, as one of God's agents, has the authority and power in the secular dimensions of life to ensure that individuals and groups—including religious communities and their agencies—adhere to the civil law. The churches and their agencies are often subject to the same legislative, judicial, and administrative provisions which affect other groups in society. But Lutheran churches will claim treatment or consideration by government different from that granted to voluntary, benevolent, eleemosynary, and educational nonprofit organizations when necessary to assure free exercise of religion. The claim for special treatment must be well founded—and the government's responses to such claims must be evenhanded, so as not to favor one type of religion or worship over another. We would maintain that government exceeds its authority when it seeks to define, determine, or otherwise influence the churches' decisions concerning their nature, mission and ministries, doctrines, worship, and other responses to God—except in critical instances, which must be considered on a case-by-case basis and which may involve church infringements of basic human rights.

Functional Interaction

However, the Lutheran churches maintain that in pursuing a joint concern for the common good, church and government can interact functionally in areas where cooperation assists in the maintenance of good order, the protection and extension of civil rights, the establishment of social justice and equality of opportunity, the promotion of the general welfare and the advancement of the dignity of all persons. This principle underscores the Lutheran view that God rules both the civil and spiritual dimensions of life, making it appropriate for churches and government to relate creatively and responsibly to each other.

In this functional interaction, the government may conclude that efforts and programs of the churches provide services of broad social benefit. In such instances and within the limits of the law, the government may offer and the church may accept funding and various other forms of assistance to furnish the services. Functional interaction also includes the role of the churches in informing persons about, advocating for, and speaking publicly on issues and proposals related to social justice and human rights. From the Lutheran perspective, the church has the task of addressing God's Word to its own activities and to the government. And the United States Constitution guarantees the right of the churches to communicate concerns to the public and to the government.

This is our conceptual framework for discussing church-state issues, one which does not provide easy "yes" or "no" answers to the difficult questions about the relationship between the two institutions.

Problems in Church-State Relations

The fact that we can have a hearing like this, where representatives of religious organizations and government can freely exchange views about the state of religious liberty, says much about the quality of church-state relations in this country. The strong differences of opinion on key issues among various religious groups testifying here reveals the diversity of religious beliefs in this country. It underscores the difficulties in developing one governmental policy or practice which accommodates all religious views and the necessity for government to maintain a truly evenhanded neutrality among all faith groups.

The Lutheran churches have identified a number of areas where church and government are in tension. Often these issues span both Republican and Democratic administrations, and are a by-product of differing understandings of responsibilities and rights of the two institutions. Noting that it is necessary for the churches to clarify for the government their position in this area, the Lutheran churches in 1979 held a consultation on "The Nature of the Church and Its Relationship With Government." It was occasioned by a number of instances in which the Lutheran churches perceived increased government encroachment on the churches' rights—instances which would result in government entanglement in religion and infringement of the free exercise of religion. . . . I would like to now focus attention on several current issues, where we see significant church-state difficulties.

Integrated Auxiliaries

From the perspective of the Lutheran churches I represent, one of the most persistent church-state problems relates to the Internal Revenue Service's (IRS) definition of an "integrated auxiliary" of a church. Through this definition the government is defining by regulation what is, or is not, an integral part of the church's mission.

Prior to 1969, most religious organizations, including churches and their related agencies, were exempted from filing informational returns with the IRS. The Tax Reform Act of 1969, however, stipulated that all organizations exempt from taxation under Section 501 (a) of the Tax Code would have to file an annual informational Form 990 return—except churches, "their integrated auxiliaries," conventions and associations of churches, the exclusively religious activities of any religious order and exempt organizations with gross receipts under $5,000 annually. The law involves the reporting of information; no payment of taxes is involved.

The problem for the IRS since 1969 has been to define "integrated auxiliaries," since that term had no legal meaning and no common definition among religious groups. In February 1976, the IRS issued proposed regulations which had the net effect of providing for all churches a single and extremely narrow definition of religious mission. Protests by a number of religious organizations led to some modifications in the "final" regulations issued in January 1977, but the regulations continue to be offensive to our mission. Explicitly excluded from the definition of "integrated auxiliaries" are church-related hospitals, orphanages, homes for the elderly, colleges, universities and elementary schools, although elementary and secondary schools are exempt from filing.

The heart of the issue is that the regulation on "integrated auxiliaries" seeks to impose on the churches a definition of "religious" and "church" which the churches cannot accept theologically, one which constitutes an unwarranted intrusion by the government into the affairs of the churches. The narrow definition introduces confusion within the churches and their agencies and institutions. It also leads the government to attempt other intrusions into the activities of the churches and church-related agencies and institutions.

Our churches would probably not object to the disclosure of most of the information required by Form 990 by those agencies and institutions of the church whose ministries appear to have counterparts in the public sphere, if such requirement or disclosure were not predicated upon a denial that those ministries are an integral part of the churches' mission. But the churches do object on principle to having any of their ministries, including their agencies and institutions, be treated as "not religious." These agencies and institutions perform ministries which are essential to the churches' mission and must not be put in a different category from the strictly sacerdotal functions of the churches. . . .

This may seem like merely a technical issue, but it is vitally important to the Lutheran churches. It is so important that they have challenged this regulation in the courts. A negative decision in the U.S. District Court, District of Minnesota, Fourth Division, is currently being appealed by those church bodies.

Government Efforts to Limit the Church's Ministry of Advocacy

The Lutheran churches firmly believe that advocacy for justice is an integral part of their mission. We have consistently resisted in principle the "substantiality test" currently in the IRS Code, as it applies to the advocacy activities of churches. We would maintain that such a test unfairly penalizes, through the threat of loss of tax exemption, those churches which regard public advocacy as part of their mission. Moreover, the effect of this test is to give preferred status, in violation of the Establishment Clause of the First Amendment, to those churches which do not participate actively in the debate on public policy. . . .

The Lutheran churches I represent believe firmly that government funds should be used expressly for the purposes Congress intends. Our social service agencies, which are often channels for federal funds to provide service to the aged, the disabled, refugees, and other persons in need, understand the importance of accountability in the use of those funds. The Lutheran churches engage in these supporting activities because social service is part of the church's mission—and in these instances, society benefits when churches and their agencies "functionally interact" with government, assisting the government in carrying out activities it has established to enhance the common good. We realize that we must be held accountable for the use of federal monies—and comply willingly with reasonable accounting and reporting requirements which ensure that that is the case. When our agencies engage in advocacy, which is also part of the mandate, they use their own funds and do *not* use any governmental funds for that purpose.

But the pending proposals, some of which have grown out of an effort to "defund the left," are overly broad, would have a chilling effect on legitimate communications between non-profits and government, and have no compelling government interest to justify their enactment. . . .

To varying degrees, such proposals would restrict the freedom of the church to speak to its members, using its own money, and to petition government—actions which are protected under the U.S. Constitution. Again, it would also favor unconstitutionally those churches which do not consider public advocacy to be part of their mission.

Government Regulation

Lutheran churches have consistently objected to governmental regulation of their educational institutions and social service agencies when such regulation violates due process, exceeds statutory authority, or infringes on First Amendment guarantees. In this process, we emphasize our solidarity with both secular and religious members of the voluntary sector and invoke the Free Exercise clause of the First Amendment as the basis for objection to regulation only when there is a *bona fide* constitutional question at stake. We do not attempt to insulate the institutional church from legitimate regulation which contributes to the common good by indiscriminately charging violations of religious liberty. The Lutheran churches analyze regulations on a case-by-case basis and develop positions which reflect their commitment to religious freedom as well as government regulation which protects the public's health, safety, and welfare.

For example, on the issue of the IRS' role vis-a-vis private school desegregation, we assert that a religious organization running an educational institution, like other tax-exempt organizations, cannot claim the exempt status and at the same time operate contrary to established public policy on racial discrimination. However, while we would acknowledge the right of the government to revoke the tax exempt status of schools which discriminate, judgments must be made on the basis of facts within a framework of due process. Presumptions on general circumstances of external conditions are inadequate for this purpose. Thus, in 1978, we were in the position of supporting the intent of IRS activity, in this area, while vehemently opposing the specific procedure proposed, since it did not meet these criteria; thereafter we supported revised regulations which we felt met our concerns about due process.

This example illustrates our approach to dealing with government regulation. Recognizing the government's interest in providing quality education for all children, we generally have no conceptual problem with reasonable certification requirements for our religious schools—as long as those requirements are not capricious or do not restrict the religious freedom of the school. Our social service agencies generally have no problem with state or federal regulations intended to protect the public health, safety and welfare—but they may have serious problems with specific regulations, which may be burdensome, unnecessary, intrusive, or punitive.

Government Establishment of Religion

In recent months, the debate over prayer in public schools has intensified. The Lutheran churches I represent would probably differ from many who will be testifying before this committee, since they have consistently supported the 1962/1963 Supreme Court decision prohibiting state-mandated prayer and Bible reading in public schools. The Lutheran churches have maintained that such a practice is unnecessary from a religious point of view. We believe that God is active in the educational process; government is fulfilling its legitimate responsibility for universal public education, and we see no need to "put God back in that process" since He has never been removed from it. The responsibility for religious education and worship rests with the family and the church—not the government.

It is important, however, that the schools maintain a wholesome neutrality among religious groups, not favoring one over the other and not denigrating religion generally. Parents and churches need to work closely with local school boards to maintain the quality of education in this and a range of areas. But it is just not appropriate for schools to have compulsory prayer of any kind, since that would put the state in the position of favoring one sort of religious practice over another—even if that religious practice would be "non-denominational" in character. Many Lutherans would have real problems with their children being encouraged, either directly or indirectly, to pray such "non-denominational" prayers, which they feel would water down the strength of their religious witness—and that of other faith groups. Lutherans, believing that all prayers must be made "in the name of Jesus," would object to having their children daily taught to pray without that understanding. From their theological perspective, non-denomination prayer *would* hurt the religious development of their children.

From our theological perspective, prayer in public school is not necessary and is potentially harmful. From a public policy viewpoint, it causes divisiveness in the community and results in significant restrictions on the freedom of religion of minority faith groups. It is not enough to say that a child can leave the classroom—when adults are well aware of the peer pressure that can undermine even the most careful of parental instruction. Protecting the religious liberty of *all* students in our public schools, whether they are Lutherans, Mormons, Jews, or members of newer religious sects is vital to the good of the nation as a whole.

86

Our concerns about the divisiveness and potential infringements of religious liberty which could occur when religious practices are conducted in public schools is the foundation for our reservations about "equal access" legislation. We would assert that religious speech should be afforded the constitutional protection it merits, also in the public schools. And in current court cases, specific instances where freedom of religion may have been abridged are being tested. But we are also concerned that legislative measures designed to remedy such abuses must not be so broadly drawn as to open the door to a range of religious activities being held in schools during the school day—activities which could result in sectarian divisiveness or in a situation which impressionable children could be evangelized or proselytized contrary to the wish of their parents, who are sending them to public schools because of the requirement of the law.

Conclusion

There are other church-state issues which are of concern to us, such as IRS/CIA/FBI impersonation of ministers in investigations, situations relating to civil disobedience by church members on issues of conscience, and restrictions on charitable solicitation by local units of government. And our state affiliates, I'm sure, could raise other concerns about church-government relations on the state and local levels. This hearing underscores the importance of continuing dialogue between churches and Congress—and between the churches and such agencies as IRS and OMB—to develop the groundwork for resolving such difficulties. . . .

The interreligious community, as well as the Lutheran churches, are engaged in continuing discussions on these issues. In 1981, 300 delegates attended a two-day conference on "Government Intervention in Religious Affairs." More than 90 percent of all of the organized religious groups in this nation sent representatives—the most inclusive religious gathering in the history of the United States. . . . In sharing common concerns, these religious groups have noted that, although some religious prejudice has been overcome, the nation still has a way to go in overcoming such prejudice vis-a-vis newer religious groups. In addition, for many mainline religious groups, tensions in the church-state area often arise from government regulation which may, in specific instances, pose a threat to their carrying out works of mercy and justice. They do not sense a sinister plot against religion by government, but a growing government entanglement in their affairs—an entanglement which sometimes occurs with little reason or cause. In continuing congressional dialogue on church-government tensions, input by those organizations is essential.

CHURCH/STATE
SEPARATION

EXCLUDING RELIGION
FROM PUBLIC LIFE

Herbert W. Titus

Herbert W. Titus presented the following testimony in his capacity as vice president for Academic Affairs, Dean and Professor of Law in the School of Public Policy at the CBN University in Virginia Beach, Virginia. CBN University is closely affiliated with the Christian Broadcasting Network, Inc., founded by televangelist Pat Robertson.

Points to Consider:

1. The author describes the religious freedom battle as "a war between two faiths." Describe the participants in this "war."
2. How did the Founding Fathers define religious freedom?
3. Why does the author believe that the courts' rulings do not reflect the faith of our forefathers?
4. Compare and contrast religious liberty and the faith of our Founding Fathers with religious liberty and the faith of scholars and judges.

Excerpted from testimony of Herbert W. Titus before the Senate Subcommittee on the Constitution of the Senate Committee on the Judiciary, June 26, 1984.

We face an enemy who, in the name of separation of church and state, seeks to exclude religion totally from the public affairs of the nation.

A War Between Two Faiths

We are at war over religious freedom in America. It is a war between two faiths. On the one side of the battle are those who believe that our constitutional guarantees of religious freedom are God-given, fixed, and governed by the words and intent of our forefathers who wrote the Constitutions of the United States and of the fifty states. On the other side are those who believe that our religious freedoms are man-invented, evolving, and authoritatively defined by the judges who sit on the highest courts of the land.

While the major battleground in this war is the United States Supreme Court, skirmishes have been taking place in the lower federal courts and in the state and local courts across the nation. Other battles have occupied legislative bodies and executive offices and agencies at the local, state, and national level. Moreover, they have been waged before school boards, in classrooms, in newspapers and magazines, over television, and even in the churches.

On each battleground, we who cherish the liberties of our forefathers are fighting on two fronts. On one front, we face an enemy who, in the name of separation of church and state, seeks to exclude religion totally from the public affairs of the nation. . . .

In the name of freedom from the "establishment of religion," these enemies of true religious freedom call for total exclusion of religion from all public life. That call for total exclusion rejects the original purpose of the Establishment Clause. The first United States Congress, author of the First Amendment of the Constitution, without hesitation asked President George Washington to issue a national declaration of the public day of "Thanksgiving and Prayer." In response, and approximately six months into his first term of office, President Washington issued the first National Thanksgiving Proclamation which reads, in part:

> Whereas it is the duty of all nations to acknowledge the providence of Almighty God, to obey His will, to be grateful for His benefits, and humbly to implore His protection and favor. . . Now, therefore, I do recommend and assign Thursday, the 26th day of November next, to be devoted by people of these States to the service of that great and glorious Being . . . And also that we may then unite in most humbly offering our prayers and supplications to the great Lord and Ruler of nations, and beseech Him to pardon our national and other transgressions. . . .

> ## CHURCH AND POLITICS
>
> *The separation of church and state means the separation of the church as an institution from the state as an institution, so that neither controls the other. The separation of church and state does not mean the separation of religious values from the political process.*
>
> *James O. Watkins,* Presbyterian Survey

Both our first Congress and our first president knew that proclamations and other statements that encouraged religion did not constitute an "establishment" of religion prohibited by the Constitution.

On the second battlefront, we face an enemy who, in the name of compelling state interest, seeks to reduce religion and religious liberty to a puny self-centered claim of conscientious objection. Congress repealed its fifty-year commitment that exempted non-profit organizations from the social security employment tax. Now churches, religious organizations, and other like employers must pay a tax on the "privilege" of hiring people to assist them to proclaim the truth and otherwise to carry out their ministries. Allowing an exemption favoring only a few who are conscientiously opposed to the social security system, Congress, because of a so-called "compelling interest" to find additional money to save a financially ailing social security system, has for the first time in its history levied a direct tax on the churches of America.

This drive toward total control has not been confined to Congress nor to economic matters. In state after state, legislatures have steadily expanded their control over education. Just this year, for example, the Virginia House of Delegates enacted a law extending state regulation of education into the home allowing for only one exception favoring those few students and parents whose religious beliefs require home education without such control. In the name of a "compelling interest" to mold its citizenry as it thinks best, Virginia seeks to capture the hearts and minds of the children from their parents. . . .

If this war on these two fronts is to be won by those who believe in the heritage of religious freedom left by our forefathers, then we must decisively reject the political and legal faith that today dominates the courts, the legislatures, the executive offices, the media, and the classrooms in America, and return to the faith of our fathers.

Religious Liberty and the Faith of Our Fathers

At the heart of religious liberty, as understood by our nation's Fathers, was their definition of religion and the declaration of its jurisdictional

immunity from state interference as exemplified by section 16 of the June 12, 1776, Virginia Bill of Rights:

> That religion, or the duty which we owe to our Creator, and the manner of discharging it, can be directed only by reason and conviction, not by force or violence; and, therefore, all men are equally entitled to the free exercise of religion, according to the dictates of conscience. . . .

In his famous "Memorial and Remonstrance on the Religious Rights of Man," James Madison, speaking in opposition to proposed state legislation to levy a tax in order to support teachers of the Christian religion, explained this constitutional text as follows:

> We remonstrate against said Bill, . . . Because we hold it for a fundamental and undeniable truth, 'that religion or the duty which we owe to our Creator and the manner of discharging it, can be directed only by reason and conviction, not by force or violence.' The religion then of every man must be left to the conviction and conscience of every man; and it is the right of every man to exercise it as these may dictate. This right is in its nature an unalienable right. It is unalienable; because the opinions of men, depending only on the evidence contemplated by their own minds, cannot follow the dictates of other men; it is unalienable also; because what is here a right towards men, is a duty towards the Creator.

It is the duty of every man to render to the Creator such homage, and such only, as he believes to be acceptable to him. This duty is precedent both in order of time and degree of obligation to the claims of Civil Society.

To Madison, and his fellow colleagues (including Jefferson), religious freedom was a God-given right, fixed and recognized by the Constitution. This view of religion presupposed a Creator from whom such rights were derived. This creationist world-view, in turn, shaped the definition of religion embraced by Madison and his congressional colleagues in formulating the First Amendment. Hence, to remain true to the original intent of the Framers of the First Amendment, one cannot examine the religious rights guaranteed thereby on the basis of Darwinian, evolutionist methodology. To the contrary, the word "religion" was used to recognize that the Creator had ordained a legal order that pre-existed all civil societies, including the unalienable right to perform those duties owed exclusively to the Creator free from civil government interference. . . .

Given the jurisdictional boundary set by the two religion clauses, the Framers constructed a scheme of civil government which was designed to avoid any conflict between God and Caesar. They allowed to appeal to any "compelling state interest" to justify government interference into any activity that belonged exclusively to God; at the same time, they rejected any argument for "religious neutrality" to prevent government regulation of activities outside that exclusive authority. Thus, a citizen would never be forced to choose between obeying his duty to his Creator or his obligations under the law of the civil authorities. Because the Framers believed that these duties had been forever fixed by an all-knowing and benevolent Creator, they had confidence that America would steer a well-charted course between the Scylla of religious anarchy and the Charybdis of religious totalitarianism.

Religious Liberty and the Faith of the Scholars and the Judges

Beginning with the mid-nineteenth century, America's scholars became increasingly dissatisfied with the legal and political faith of their nation's founders. Under the influence of Darwin's new evolutionary theory about the origin of the universe and of man, American jurisprudence shifted to a new assumption that judges did not discover law, but that they, in fact, made it.

This legal philosophy is today's conventional wisdom taught in almost every law school in America. So widely held is this view that Laurence Tribe, professor of law at Harvard, stated with confidence and without discussion in the preface to his treatise on American Constitutional Law: "The Constitution is an intentionally incomplete, often deliberately indeterminate structure for the participatory evolution of political ideas and governmental practices."

92

Under this view, law, having been "liberated" from fixed principles, has become subject to judges who make decisions according to changing social values and changing factual circumstances. The fixed law that originally guaranteed our religious freedoms has been discarded in favor of a new set of fleeting rules invented by judges.

Since 1971, the United States Supreme Court has articulated a three-part test governing the constitutionality of religious claims under the First Amendment's Establishment Clause. *Lemon v. Kurtzman,* 403 U.S. 602, 612-613 (1971). At the heart of this test is the Court's distinction between the "secular" and the "religious." Although the Court has never carefully explained this distinction, it has consistently followed a pattern of decisions that reflects the definition offered by Justice John Paul Stevens in his concurring and dissenting opinion in *Wolman v. Walters,* 433 U.S. 263 (1978): "The distinction between the religious and secular is a fundamental one. To quote from Clarence Darrow's argument in the Scopes case: 'The realm of religion . . . is where knowledge leaves off, and faith begins. . . .'"

This evolutionary faith, that the religious freedom clauses separated out two kinds of "subject matters" and allocated one, "science," to the state, and another, "religion," to the church, has led the courts to exclude all God-revealed knowledge from the public school classroom. For example, Justice Tom Clark in *Abington School District v. Schempp,* 374 U.S. 203 (1963) ruled that the Bible may be taught in the public schools, but only if it is not presented as the Word of God. Following in these footsteps, a lower federal court judge has ruled that the creationist view of the origin of the world and of man may not be taught in the public schools because, based upon revealed truth, it is necessarily religious. *McLean v. Arkansas Bd. of Education,* No. LRC 81-322 (E.D. Ark. 1982)

Moreover, the Supreme Court has held that the posting of the Ten Commandments upon a public school classroom wall violates the Establishment Clause because the first four of those commandments are necessarily "religious" while only the last six could possibly be "secular." *Stone v. Graham,* 449 U.S. 39, 41-42 (1980). By this decision the Court has suggested that some topics, like belief in God, must be totally excluded from the public school classroom because such a belief is not empirically verifiable.

Moreover, the Court has claimed that it must separate the "religious" from the "secular" in order to achieve its own goal of religious neutrality in the public affairs of the nation. . . . While the Court has rightfully rejected these efforts to eliminate all religious values from the law, it has pursued its policy of neutrality in the public schools to the complete and total exclusion of this country's Christian heritage from the public schools. A position such as this can be "neutral" only if one adopts the Court's assumption that God need not be consulted in man's search for truth. That was not the faith of our forefathers. . . .

Conclusion

In the early history of the Christian church, the religious department of the Roman Empire commanded the apostles to stop teaching in the name of Jesus. Having been taught well by their Master to render to Caesar only that which belonged to Caesar, the church fathers answered: "We ought to obey God rather than men." Acts 5:29.

This biblical lesson of jurisdiction inspired America's forefathers to write a constitutional guarantee of religious freedom that would protect themselves and future generations from civil government tyranny. Only if that jurisdictional principle remains fixed and absolute in American constitutional law will the people remain free. Changing constitutional principles in order to accommodate changes in circumstances and values does not yield "a living Constitution" as some believe. To the contrary, adhering strictly to the original terms, neither adding to nor subtracting from them, is the only assurance of true liberty and prosperity. It is as Moses spoke to the people of Israel: "Keep. . .the words of this covenant, and do them that ye may prosper in all that ye do." (Deuteronomy 29:9). . .

The American people must vigilantly pray for and select leaders who will make it their commitment to interpret and apply the constitutional text according to its historic meaning rooted in the Framer's faith in God.

WHAT IS RELIGIOUS BIAS?

This activity may be used as an individualized study guide for students in libraries and resource centers or as a discussion catalyst in small group and classroom discussions.

The capacity to recognize an author's point of view is an essential reading skill. The skill to read with insight and understanding involves the ability to detect different kinds of opinions or bias. Sex bias, race bias, ethnocentric bias, political bias, and religious bias are five basic kinds of opinions expressed in editorials and all literature that attempts to persuade. They are briefly defined below.

---

5 Kinds of Editorial Opinion or Bias

SEX BIAS—The expression of dislike for and/or feeling of superiority over a person because of gender or sexual preference

RACE BIAS—The expression of dislike for and/or feeling of superiority over a racial group

ETHNOCENTRIC BIAS—The expression of a belief that one's own group, race, religion, culture, or nation is superior. Ethnocentric persons judge others by their own standards and values.

POLITICAL BIAS—The expression of political opinions and attitudes about domestic or foreign affairs

RELIGIOUS BIAS—The expression of a religious belief or attitude

---

Guidelines (Part A)

Evaluate the statements below by using the method indicated.

Check ✓ the letter [R] in front of any sentence that is an example of religious opinion or bias. Check ✓ the letter [N] in front of any sentence that is not an example of religious opinion or bias.

☐ R ☐ N 1. Churches should not be in the business of using the coercive power of the state to enforce their versions of what is moral; similarly, the state should not assume the functions of the church in preaching or evangelizing, or determine for the church what is or is not part of its mission.

☐ R ☐ N 2. The same principle that requires government to make a reasonable accommodation to religion as part of society requires religion to make a reasonable accommodation of government.

☐ R ☐ N 3. Our first Congress and our first president knew that proclamations and other statements that encouraged religion did not constitute an "establishment" of religion prohibited by the Constitution.

☐ R ☐ N 4. There is a growing notion that government has the duty to inspect, register, and certify religion as it does meat.

☐ R ☐ N 5. The founders of this nation never intended for this to be a nation which was neutral toward God.

☐ R ☐ N 6. While it may be arrogant to talk about forming a "Moral Majority," it is at least within the boundaries of pluralism, while talk of forming a "Christian Nation" is not.

☐ R ☐ N 7. The First Amendment does not teach the separation of church and state.

☐ R ☐ N 8. Private and church-related schools, hospitals, homes, and other institutions usually do as good a job as public institutions.

☐ R ☐ N 9. The church firmly believes that advocacy for justice is an integral part of its mission.

☐ R ☐ N 10. The idea that religion and politics don't mix was invented by the Devil to keep Christians from running their own country.

☐ R ☐ N 11. Church bodies and other groups of Christians have both the right and the responsibility to make their views known on public policy issues.

☐ R ☐ N 12. America was founded as a Christian nation. Our problems will continue to afflict us until we put the Bible back into politics.

96

Guidelines (Part B)

1. See how many factual statements you can locate in the 12 items listed above.

2. Make up one-sentence statements that would be an example of each of the following: *sex bias, race bias, ethnocentric bias, political bias, and religious bias.*

3. See how many statements reflecting political bias you can locate in the 12 items listed above.

CHAPTER 3

RELIGION AND EDUCATION

RELIGION
AND EDUCATION

SECULARISTS CHASE RELIGION
OUT OF EDUCATION

Virgil C. Blum

Virgil C. Blum, S. J. wrote the following article in his capacity as professor emeritus of political science at Marquette University and as founder and president of the Catholic League for Religious and Civil Rights. His article appeared in Crisis, *a journal of lay Catholic opinion and a publication of the Brownson Institute, Notre Dame, Indiana.*

Points to Consider:

1. What is meant by the secularization of public schools?
2. Summarize the findings of the Vitz research.
3. Define "Secularism."
4. By banning the teaching of religion, have public schools established religious neutrality or have they established Secularism?

Virgil C. Blum, "Secularism in Public Schools," *Crisis,* March 1987, pp. 22-24. Reprinted with permission from the March 1987 issue of *Crisis* (P.O. Box 1006, Notre Dame, IN 46556).

The ignoring of religion by the schools inevitably conveys to the children a negative suggestion. . . . that religion is negligible, or unimportant, or irrelevant to the main business of life.

One of the most hotly debated issues of the day is whether the religion of the public schools is Secularism. When the Supreme Court forbade the teaching of the traditional religions in public schools, did it, in doing so, establish religious neutrality? Or did it effectively establish a new religion called Secularism?

Teaching of Religion is Banned

In compliance with the Court's decisions, most public schools have banned the teaching of religion. In doing so, they have effectively suppressed the teaching of religiously-grounded moral values. This was the rather startling finding of a research team, directed by Jonathan Friendly and was reported in the *New York Times* (December 1, 1985). Friendly wrote: "At a time of increased pressure from top federal officials and some educators and parents groups for public schools to teach moral values, many educators in the New York area say they deliberately avoid trying to tell students what is ethically right and wrong." Friendly continued: "Values are much less discussed in public schools now than they were in the late 1960s, educators say. And specific courses in values or religion or democracy, once popular in high school curriculums, are now rare, in part because they are controversial and in part because there are few teachers trained to give them."

For these reasons, courses in values are rare, indeed. But more important, such courses are rare because they challenge the accepted religion of Secularism. Dr. Robert Laber, the assistant superintendent of curriculum in Darien, Connecticut, put it bluntly: "It's outside the scope of our charge to teach moral values."

Teaching of Morals is Prohibited

According to Jonathan Friendly, the teaching of morals is not only "outside the charge" of public education, it is prohibited. He wrote:

City and suburban schools alike forbid teachers to advocate personal values, particularly on topics of current controversy, such as abortion or disarmament. As a result, substance-abuse programs. . .do not teach abstention (a moral value) from drugs and alcohol as much as they teach a thinking process that would lead students to decide against drugs and drinking, the educators said.

In other words, public school teachers are forbidden to advocate such religiously-grounded moral values as freedom, justice, equality, and democracy. Neither can they teach students the moral, social, and economic evils of drugs, alcohol, and pre-marital sex. Nor can they teach students such moral values as recognizing the dignity of man, the sanctity of life, and the importance of responsible social relations.

The Secularization of Public Schools

This is what is meant by the secularization of our public schools: the suppression not only of the teaching of religion but also of religiously-grounded moral values. Forbidding the teaching of such values is virtually the same as teaching that those values are false, or at least irrelevant to man's affairs. But Secularists in state education have taken a big step beyond suppressing the teaching of religiously-grounded moral values. They have effectively censored from textbooks virtually all references to the place of religion in Western civilization and in American history.

Dr. Paul Vitz, professor of psychology at New York University, headed a research team that conducted seven different assessments, covering the 90 textbooks which are most widely used in America's public schools. Entitled "Religion and Traditional Values in Public School Textbooks: An Empirical Study," the study's purpose was to determine the values that are being taught to today's students.

Consider treatment of religion in the sixth grade "world culture" texts from ten social studies series. In these texts, the long history of the Jewish people is neglected. Further, Jesus of Nazareth, indisputably one of the most important figures in history, is almost totally neglected. He is not mentioned at all in four books, and three others give Him but scanty mention. Only one book has any significant coverage of the rise of Christianity.

Most astonishing is the neglect of Protestantism in the texts. While three do not even mention the Reformation, those that do give it an extremely superficial treatment. Only two texts refer to the theological issues that inspired the great religious leaders during that period. . . .

Mission Schools of Secularism

Finally, the New York University team undertook the examination of religion and values as found in the third and sixth grade reading texts. They reviewed every story and article—a total of 670 items—in the eleven texts for each of the third and sixth grades. The team made a shocking discovery: "There is not one story or article in all these books in which the central motivation or major content deals with religion. No character has a primary religious motivation. . . . No informative article dealt with religion as a primary subject worthy of treatment." Even more amazing, 16 of the 22 books contain no reference to God, Christianity, or Judaism.

The evidence of the Vitz research is compelling and profoundly disturbing. Most public school students—60 to 80 percent depending on grade level—must use texts which have been censored of virtually all references to religion. Furthermore, this censorship occurs most often in those courses that are most important—on both the intellectual and the imaginative levels—in shaping the moral values of students.

When they were founded in the middle of the nineteenth century, the public schools were firmly committed to the Christian religion, or at least to Christian moral values. Today, they have become the mission schools of Secularism.

Secularism Defined

What, then, is Secularism? The well-known Protestant theologian, Robert McAfee Brown of Stanford University, is quite candid that it is, in essence, a kind of faith: "Secularism is itself a 'faith.' The *object* and *content* of Secularism's faith may be, and indeed are, very different from the object and content of the faith possessed by a Catholic or a Protestant or a Jew, but a faith it is and a religion it is." Former Harvard President Nathan M. Pusey confirmed this view when he told a graduating class that Secularism has "itself become a *faith* and raised a hope that man can through his own effort—without God—solve all the remaining problems which stand between him and a secular paradise on earth."

Sir Walter Moberly, a British scholar, underscored the pedagogical impact of so-called religious neutrality on children. In *The Crisis in the University* he observed:

> On the fundamental religious issue (the existence of God), the modern [school] intends to be, and supposes it is, neutral, but it is not. Certainly it neither inculcates nor expressly repudiates belief in God. But it does what is far more deadly than open rejection; it ignores Him. . . . It is in this sense that the [school] today is atheistic.

Religion Becomes Unimportant

Dr. Luther A. Weigle, former dean of the Yale Divinity School, agreed when he said, "The ignoring of religion by the schools inevitably conveys to the children a negative suggestion. . . . It is natural for them to conclude that religion is negligible, or unimportant, or irrelevant to the main business of life."

Dr. Henry P. Van Dusen, former president of Union Theological Seminary, emphasized the essential role of religion in education in *God in Education:*

> Religion is the determinative principle in the educational process as a whole, affecting vitally and decisively the over-all philosophy and content of the curriculum and of its every part, reflecting religion's basic premise that God is the ultimate Ground of Truth in relation to which every segment of knowledge and all particular truths must be oriented.

Weigle maintained that not to teach religion is to teach that religion is irrelevant:

> A system of public education that gives no place to religion is not in reality neutral, but exerts an influence, unintentional though it

is, against religion. . . .The omission of religion from the public schools conveys a condemnatory suggestion to the children. . . .

Writing in *Commentary,* the late Dr. Will Herberg, former professor of philosophy and culture at Drew University, concurred: "Today the spirit of public school education is, by and large, Secularist, and even militantly so."

Charles Clayton Morrison, former editor of *Christian Century,* noted this fact with evident pain when he wrote: "The public school is confessedly and deliberately secular. I am bound, therefore, to lay at the doorstep of our educational system the prime responsibility of the decline of religion and the steady advance of Secularism, another name for atheism, in America society." Answering those critics who say that it is the function of the churches, not the schools, to teach religion, Clayton continued: "Protestant children in public schools are under an influence with which the churches cannot compete and which they cannot counteract. The public school presents the church with a generation of youth whose minds have been cast in a secular mold."

Schools are not Religiously Neutral

Scholars no longer espouse the myth that our public schools are religiously neutral. They recognize that public schools now teach the religion of Secularism, and that this teaching is destructive of the Christian and Jewish beliefs of our children. But is Secularism *legally* a religion?

In the *Torcaso* case (1961), the Supreme Court said that "among religions in this country which do not teach what would generally be considered a belief in the existence of God are Buddhism, Taoism, Ethical Culture, Secular Humanism and others." According to this decision, Secularism is a religion under the First Amendment, and has all the rights and liberties of our theistic religions.

And the Supreme Court conceded in the *Everson* case (1947) that Secularism is in fact the religion of the public schools. "Our public school," it said, "is organized on the premises that secular education can be isolated from all religious teaching so that the school can inculcate all needed temporal knowledge. . . ."

The establishment of Secularism in public schools does indeed make them the mission schools of Secularism, with unlimited opportunities to proselytize. In 1983 the *Humanist,* the journal of the American Humanist Association, published a prize-winning essay which expressed the conviction that "the battle for humankind's future must be waged and won in the public school classroom by teachers who correctly perceive their role as the proselytizers of a new faith."

The findings of the Vitz and Friendly research teams clearly show how effectively the Secularist proselytizers are carrying out this mission. Sir Walter Moberly made this point most emphatically:

It is a fallacy to suppose that by omitting a subject you teach nothing about it. On the contrary you teach that it is to be omitted, and that it is therefore a matter of secondary importance. And you teach this not openly and explicitly, which would invite criticism; you simply take it for granted and thereby insinuate it silently, insidiously, and all but irresistibly.

When we teach our children that religion is to be omitted from their education, we destroy the very foundations of our moral values. . . .

Destroying Cultural Foundations

This forcible indoctrination of our public school children is having a most detrimental effect on our society, argues the late English historian Christopher Dawson, while lecturing at Harvard University. He exclaimed in *Jubilee* magazine that "the existence of this deadening blanket of Secularist conformity which is stifling the spiritual and intellectual life of modern culture" is "a new threat to human freedom which is more far-reaching and profound than anything the past has known."

"The socialization and secularization of education," wrote Dawson in *The Crisis of Western Education,* "has created an immense professionalized organ for the creation of moral and intellectual uniformity." This is the ultimate suppression of freedom, the uniformity of the graveyard.

Our forefathers built America on the principles of pluralism and freedom, not on the totalitarian principles of enforced conformity and uniformity of the graveyard. "The American way of life," wrote Dawson, "was built on a threefold tradition of freedom—political, economic, and religious—and if the new Secularist forces were to subjugate these freedoms to a monolithic technological order, it would destroy the foundations on which American culture was based."

The Supreme Court stated these same principles of freedom most emphatically in the *Barnette* flag-salute case: "If there is any fixed star in our constitutional constellation, it is that no official, high or petty, can prescribe what shall be orthodox in politics, nationalism, religion, or other matters of opinion or force citizens to confess by word or act their faith therein."

Yet, by establishing the religion of Secularism in our public schools, the government has in fact prescribed what shall be orthodox in religion and morality, and is forcing our children to confess their faith therein.

RELIGION
AND EDUCATION

THE RELIGIOUS RIGHT
FORCE EDUCATION
FROM THE CLASSROOM

David Saperstein and Charles Bergstrom

David Saperstein co-authored this article in his capacity as a rabbi and director of the Religious Action Center of Reform Judaism.

Charles Bergstrom co-authored this article in his capacity as a minister and executive director for governmental affairs of the Lutheran Council in the U.S.A.

Points to Consider:

1. Why are the authors against the banning of books from public schools?
2. Why are publishers and teachers avoiding the topic of religion altogether?
3. Describe the decision in *Abington Township v. Schempp.*
4. Compare and contrast the teaching *of* religion and teaching *about* religion.

The Religious Right seeks to impose its spiritual views on others by using the coercive force of government to ban books and turn the classroom into a pulpit for sectarian teachings.

On March 4, 1987, Judge Brevard Hand banned 40 textbooks from Alabama's public schools because they promoted a religion, "secular humanism."* The case arose from a systemic problem—the growing omission of discussion of religion in the textbooks and classes of public schools. Yet both the plaintiffs' account of the source of the problem and the judge's bizarre remedy miss the point. Secularists haven't chased religion from our classrooms. The Religious Right has. Banning books isn't the answer; rediscovering an educationally sound and constitutionally permissible way to teach about religion is.

Don't Teach Religion; Teach *About* It

The efforts of the Religious Right to introduce sectarian teachings into the public schools has had the paradoxical effect of depriving young Americans of knowledge about the role of religion in history and culture, and about the comparative teachings of diverse religious creeds. In the face of the fundamentalist campaign to require the teaching of "creationism" as scientific truth and to censor textbooks containing "unacceptable" descriptions of religion, many publishers have found it easier to remove any reference to religion from their textbooks, avoiding the topic of religion altogether rather than seeking to accommodate conflicting viewpoints.

Similarly, school administrators, intimidated by lawsuits and by parents who threaten to pull their children out of classes that discuss "religiously offensive" ideas, are advising teachers to steer clear of any mention of religion.

The removal of religion as a subject of study has dismayed many responsible educators, parents, and mainstream religious leaders, who strongly support the Supreme Court's stand that the public schools have the right to teach *about* religion but not to teach which religious beliefs are correct.

A Vital Distinction

In *Abington Township v. Schempp,* the 1963 decision striking down Bible-reading in public schools, the Court ruled: "It might well be said

---

*Editor's note: Judge Hand's ruling was overturned in August 1987 by a federal appeals court.

that one's education is not complete without a study of comparative religion and its relationship to the advancement of civilization. . . . Nothing that we have said here indicates that such study of Bible or of religion, when presented objectively as part of a secular program of education, may not be effected consistent with the First Amendment."

The distinction between teaching the "truth" of religion and teaching "about" religion is vital. The first introduces denominational differences and theological strife into the classroom. Teaching "about" religion allows students to study the influences that religion has had on history, culture, and values. Indeed, it is impossible to understand the development of civilization without recognizing the impact of religious beliefs and institutions. Failing to cover religion in public schools, however, implies that it is not an important element of life.

Schools Could Promote Understanding

In learning about different religions, children receive a vital component of their education. Public schools should teach about the diversity of religious traditions in America while remaining neutral on the beliefs themselves. In this way, schools can promote understanding, alleviate prejudice, and prepare students to participate in a pluralistic society. Religious beliefs themselves are the proper domain of the church, the synagogue, and the home.

Many Americans share with the Reverend Jerry Falwell and the Reverend Pat Robertson and others the goal of strengthening religious values and morality. How best to achieve it divides us sharply. The Religious Right seeks to impose its spiritual views on others by using the coercive force of government to ban books and turn the classroom into a pulpit for sectarian teachings. We reject this approach.

Cartoon by William Sanders. Reprinted with special permission of NAS, Inc.

Teaching the importance of religion's contributions to civilization does not mean that the schools should be used to promote organized prayer, devotional readings, or other practices that belong at home or in houses of worship. Teaching religion undermines our freedoms and divides our children along religious lines. Teaching about religion nourishes these freedoms and offers a genuine opportunity to endow American values with the knowledge of our nation's diverse and rich religious traditions.

RELIGION
AND EDUCATION

TEACHING RELIGION FAIRLY
WOULD BE DIFFICULT

Edd Doerr

Edd Doerr wrote the following article in his capacity as vice president of the American Humanist Association and executive director of Americans for Religious Liberty. His article appeared in The Humanist, *a publication of the American Humanist Association.*

Points to Consider:

1. How does the author describe the Vitz study?
2. Summarize the results of the Association of Supervision and Curriculum Development's report.
3. Why would fair teaching about religion be difficult?
4. How should public schools deal with the teaching of values?

Edd Doerr, "Religion in Public Education," *The Humanist,* November/December 1987, pp. 41-42. This article first appeared in *The Humanist* issue of November/December 1987 and is reprinted by permission.

Fair, factual, and adequate teaching about religion means that the teaching should be comprehensive and present a balanced picture of the bad as well as the good.

"Educators call for end of silence in nation's classrooms." That and similar newspaper headlines point up the growing "demand" for public schools to "do something" about religion. While there is little evidence for appreciable grassroots demand for teaching about religion in school, opinion polls have registered solid approval for teaching or promoting values in school. Though related in intricate ways, however, teaching about religion and promoting ethical or moral values are two very different things and pose different sets of problems for educators.

Religion in Public Education

It is true that religion is not adequately dealt with in public schools (or, it might be added, in the media or anywhere else). Psychologist Paul Vitz produced a study for the Reagan administration ostensibly to document this charge, though scholars have found his work sloppy and Vitz himself has an axe to grind: he dislikes public education in principle and favors tax support of sectarian private schools. A study of textbooks by People for the American Way also found inadequate attention to religion. Meanwhile, the Alabama textbook censorship case (in which Judge Brevard Hand ruled in March 1987 that 44 textbooks slighted religion and therefore were "teaching secular humanism," a ruling overturned in August by a federal appeals court) has further highlighted the sparse treatment of religion in school.

But rather than being the result of some dark conspiracy against or hostility toward religion, the slighting of religion in public schools stems from a justifiable fear on the part of educators and textbook publishers of handling a very controversial issue, from lack of real demand for academic study of religion, and from simple lack of agreement as to precisely what should be taught.

ASCD Report and Recommendations

In the most recent development, the Association of Supervision and Curriculum Development (ASCD) has just released a report and recommendations entitled *Religion in the Curriculum*. The report deplores the slighting of religion in social studies and literature classes and notes that the Supreme Court in the 1963 *Schempp* prayer ruling said that objective, neutral, academic study of religion in public schools is both advisable and constitutional.

The ASCD report suggests that educators must be committed to pluralism and democracy, that religion is not "too hot for them to han-

111

dle in an informed, descriptive, and impartial way," that schools should respect the beliefs students bring with them from home, that teaching materials should be "accurate, objective, honest, fair, and interesting," that educators should carefully avoid usurping the religious role of the family and the family's religious institution or institutions, and that study about religion should be included in the core curriculum.

Finally, the ASCD study recommends that textbook selection committees should require in all curricular materials fair, factual, "adequate treatment of diverse religions and their roles in American and world culture and to include appropriate religious and moral themes in literary and art history anthologies"; that teachers should have both substantive and methods training to deal with religion; and that educator organizations should promote "public support for the teaching of rigorous, intellectually demanding accounts of religion in society, particularly in American society."

The ASCD recommendations are all right as far as they go. But the report does not come to grips with the enormous complexity and difficulty of the subject.

Some Thorny Subjects

Fair, factual, and adequate teaching about religion means, of course, that the teaching should be comprehensive and present a balanced picture of the bad as well as the good. In world history and, to an extent, in U.S. history, schools would have to deal with such thorny subjects as how to treat the Jewish, Christian, Muslim, and other scriptures; the sharp Catholic and non-Catholic differences over the development

Cartoon by Stein. Reprinted by permission of NEA, Inc.

of the papacy; syncretism in the history of Christianity; the extermination of the Albigensians and persecution of the Waldensians; the Inquisition; Calvin's Geneva; the religious wars after the Reformation; the many unpleasant facets of the Crusades; the wars between Christians and Muslims; the long history of anti-Semitism and other, often murderous, forms of bigotry; the role of religion in social and international tensions; the conflicts between religion and science; the religion-related "troubles" in Northern Ireland; the role of religion in French, Spanish, and other European colonizations; religion and the Vietnamese quagmire; religion and liberation theology in Latin America; and religion in the Spanish Civil War and World War II. And these are just some of the problems in world history that would require fair, factual treatment.

In U.S. history, some of the equally thorny issues would be native American religion; French and Spanish missions; the European religious background of migration to North America; the execution of Quakers in and expulsion of Anne Hutchinson from Massachusetts; the Salem witch trials; colonial establishments of religion and bigotry; revivalism; deism; anti-Catholicism; anti-Semitism; pacifism; the evolution of religious liberty and church-state separation; the history of various denominations and movements; denominations and religions founded in the United States (Christian Science, the "Campbellite" churches, Shakers, Mormonism, and new religions such as the Unification Church, Hare Krishna movement, and Scientology); deprogramming; religious utopian experiments; religion on both sides of the slavery issue; black religion; non-Western religions in the United States; nativism; the temperance movement; the controversy over evolution and other conflicts between religion and science; religion and welfare programs; contemporary church-state problems; religious conflict and abortion rights; religion, war, and conscientious objection; the modernist-fundamentalist debate; important theologians; religion and the Vietnam War; women and religion; religion and the civil rights movement; religion in public education; the relation between religion and values, daily life, and behavior; the new Religious Right and politics; the "unchurched"; and liberal religion and humanism.

Can We Handle It?

Are educators and textbook publishers ready to deal with these issues fairly and factually? Will most parents go along with factual treatment of these issues? Will religious leaders do so? At what grade levels will these issues be dealt with? As crowded as the social studies curriculum is—and critics point out that U.S. history and world history are presently poorly taught (and all too often by coaches with little interest in teaching)—where will all this vast amount of material fit?

What about teacher preparation and certification? Will schools erect firm safeguards against proselytizing or slanting of material?

The ASCD has made a good start at approaching the subject of religion in the curriculum. But it is obvious that a great deal more needs to be done.

Values Education

On the subject of values, we have another sticky issue. Schools cannot avoid teaching values, so it is a question of which values are taught. Without going into great detail, most of us should be able to agree that there are common, civilized, democratic values which can and should be taught—through example and through the curriculum. There are common values on which people of all religious and ideological persuasions should be able to agree, values embodied in the Declaration of Independence, the Constitution, the Bill of Rights, and ethical teachings of most religions and life stances.

Educators and all citizens should concern themselves with the question of values education. In teaching about religion, we should avoid rushing into something so serious without extreme caution and adequate preparation.

RELIGION
AND EDUCATION

COMPROMISING ON THE
RELIGION-IN-EDUCATION DEBATE

Charles L. Glenn

Dr. Charles L. Glenn wrote this article in his capacity as the director of the Bureau of Equal Educational Opportunity for the Massachusetts Department of Education. He is also associate pastor of the church of the Holy Spirit. His article appeared in The Christian Century, *a weekly ecumenical publication.*

Points to Consider:

1. Compare and contrast the concerns of "strict separationists" and the "Religious Right" regarding public education.
2. Why does the author consider litigation ineffective in dealing with public education conflicts?
3. Explain the term "value-free curriculum."
4. Do strongly held religious convictions inevitably conflict with our system of public education? Provide examples to support your answer.

Is there a solution to the perennial conflict over the values presented in public schools? I believe there is.

Do strongly held religious convictions inevitably conflict with our system of public education? A visitor from another planet might well conclude that they do, given the heated attacks on public schools from the "Religious Right," and the equally heated warnings by "strict separationists" that there is a plot by "zealots" to impose religious uniformity on the nation's schoolchildren.

A very grave situation indeed. . . . if true. In particular, those of us committed to public education should feel that our backs are against the wall if the commentators are reading the signs of the times correctly. And those of us who believe in respect for religious conviction in its diverse forms have further grounds for deep concern if the choices are truly "all or nothing" between an imposed orthodoxy and an education from which all religious reference has been purged.

However, I am convinced that the polemicists in both camps—the "strict separationists" and the "Religious Right"—read the signs of the times incorrectly.

Mutual Incomprehensions

A democratic polity has ample room for many shades of opinion; what it cannot well tolerate is attempts to excommunicate the opposition, to set it outside the range of permissible dialogue. The ugly aspect of the current debates is that some are attempting just such excommunication. After all, if the nation (that is, all of us) is "besieged by religious zealots" or "controlled by secular humanists," the image suggests that we shut fast the gates and unite to repel their attacks.

What seems to be excluded by the nature of the current debate is the possibility of trying to understand the intentions (however clumsily implemented) of public educators on the one hand, or the concerns of religiously conservative parents (however clumsily expressed) on the other. As a public education official and an evangelical, I have become deeply concerned about this mutual incomprehension, and am convinced that beyond the alienating rhetoric about "humanist conspiracies" there are some legitimate grievances that should, for the sake of justice and the rights of conscience, be addressed.

Battles in the Courtroom

In the name of religious liberty and of tolerance, I have found, the radical separationists are profoundly intolerant and illiberal toward religious conservatives. Such conservatives, estimated by pollster Daniel Yankelovich as one American in five, are actually somewhat marginal to the mainstream of national life, have few polished spokespersons, and are given to unsophisticated and vehement expression of their resentment about assaults on their convictions and values. This makes them an easy target, but it does not make throwing mud at them an exercise in religious liberalism.

Those who see any intrusion of religious concerns into public life as a profound threat to American democracy are having a field day with the recent federal court rulings in Tennessee and Alabama, upholding suits brought by concerned parents. . . .The Tennessee judge (in *Mozart v. Hawkins County*) ordered in November 1986 that public schools honor a request by a group of parents that their children be excused from using certain readers offensive to their religious convictions. . . .The litigation in Alabama (*Smith v. Board of School Commissioners*), resulting in an early March ruling that "secular humanism" represents an unconstitutional "establishment of religion," has been the occasion for a new round of public anguish on the part of the separationists. . . .

Respect and Accommodation

Who, then, is the aggressor? Is it "religious zealots" who are besieging the ramparts of our common life as a nation? Or do conservative Christians (and other religious groups) have some right to feel backed into a corner by the relentlessly secularizing message of the mainstream media, of the public school curriculum, of those who seek to remove every acknowledgment of religion from the public square?

The claim that religious conservatives are about to seize control of the nation and impose their religious beliefs is either cynical or paranoid; it takes seriously the fantasies of the "theonomists" and other tiny groups among the millions of evangelicals and traditional Roman Catholics who are fully committed to playing by the rules of a pluralist democracy.

118

What most religious conservatives (who may, like me, be political liberals) ask is that our convictions be treated with respect and accommodated, not that they be imposed on anyone. The American political system has in fact shown a remarkable ability, for two centuries, to find such accommodations and to allow room for minority beliefs and opinions to flourish.

Litigation is not the Answer

Although sympathizing with the parents in Tennessee and Alabama, I deplore the increasing tendency to turn to the courts to resolve such issues. It is a bad way to achieve compromise and accommodation. By casting the issues in the absolute terms of constitutional protected rights, such litigation encourages a hardening of positions on both sides. Courts tend to rule on the basis of underlying principles that, once applied, may go far beyond the original intentions of the parties, and in ways that are contrary to the interest of all (see Luke 12:58). Certainly there are many instances in which action is necessary to guarantee basic freedoms and equal protection under the law, but litigation should be the last resort, not—as too often today—the first.

The teaching of values and attitudes, of loyalties and aversions is not, it seems to me, a promising area for litigation. Inevitably it involves many fine adjustments, subtle judgments based upon the mature convictions of teachers and of parents, and their sense of responsibility for children—each of whom is unique. Such matters can neither be legislated nor ordered by a court. School life, like family life, does not flourish in an atmosphere of continual assertion of rights and grievances. . . .

A Palette of Gray

Do we really want our public schools to be pushed further and further toward the blandness of a value-free curriculum? There is overwhelming evidence, from surveys both nationally and in a number of states, that parents do not, that they seek schools for their children in which clear standards come to expression. The present competition between ideological opponents to exclude anything offensive to their religious or secularist views is a strategy of "mutual assured destruction" of values and convictions. When all the strong colors are removed from the teacher's palette we will be left with shades of gray—moral indifferentism. The parents who brought the Alabama and Tennessee suits are convinced that this process has already gone too far, yet ironically the litigation could drive it further. The effect would be devastating for public schools and for teachers and children.

Cartoon by Herblock. Reprinted with permission from *Herblock at Large* (Pantheon Books, 1987).

Can a Compromise be Reached?

It was an illusion of Horace Mann and the other reformers who shaped our educational system in conscious opposition to "sectarian" schools that a coherent "common" education could be provided by stressing only those convictions on which "men of good will" agreed. They had some excuses for their view; theirs was the age of the "evangelical united front" for social reform, and the stubborn resistance of Catholics could be seen as a short-term result of their foreignness. Unfortunately, the common beliefs and values on which the "common school" rested have been dissolved away by the acids of modernity. Humpty-Dumpty is not to be put back together, and it is inappropriate to seek to do so by using mandatory school attendance to inculcate values in children that their parents find offensive.

The January appeal filed in the Tennessee case on behalf of the school system could not be more clear in its assertion for a right to teach such values:

> The schools seek to teach students to be autonomous individuals, who can make their own judgments about moral questions. The schools believe that students should be able to evaluate and make judgments on their own, based on their experience and beliefs, not those of their teachers. . . . many of the plaintiffs' objections are directly inconsistent with the objectives of public education.

We take so much for granted the language of individual autonomy that it requires an effort to remember that there is another way of seeing the task of education, one involving exposure to a tradition representing accumulated (even divinely revealed) truth. In this view, pre-teenaged children should not be confronted with moral dilemmas in their elementary readers and encouraged to find their "own" solutions; they should be taught right from wrong by adults confident that these are absolutes.

It is not my purpose to argue for the correctness of one or the other view of education, only to note that these are issues over which reasonable people may differ, and to question whether the State has a right to impose the first approach in the face of opposition from parents. Indeed, by allowing parents to meet the compulsory school attendance requirement by sending their children to private institutions that espouse the second approach, the State tacitly acknowledges that its "compelling interest" in education is adequately served in such schools.

A Proposed Solution

Is there a solution to the perennial conflict over the values presented in public schools? I believe there is. It starts with the recognition that public schools do not need to be identical, that they can offer a variety of pedagogically legitimate approaches to common educational goals.

121

To take the example always used by those arguing for the "common school," religious tolerance can be taught without necessarily giving the message that all religious views are of equal validity. A good argument can be made, in fact, that the person who is solidly grounded in a religious identity is more free to be tolerant than another from whom differing beliefs are a threat. Catholics who graduate from Catholic schools, for example, may be more tolerant than Catholics who attended public schools.

This is not to argue that we should divide publicly supported education along denominational lines, as is the case in most Western democracies. Surveys indicate that while parents would like more choice in education, the number for whom explicitly religious instruction is a primary consideration is relatively small; most seem content to leave that to their churches and synagogues. A much greater concern, however, is the moral flavor of the school, the values by which it lives as well as those which it explicitly teaches. In this respect schools can differ greatly without going beyond what is appropriate for public education.

RELIGION
AND EDUCATION

RELIGIOUS EDUCATION
IN PUBLIC SCHOOLS:
THE CANADIAN EXAMPLE

America Magazine

The following editorial offers several examples of how Canada deals with religious education in public schools. It appeared in America, *a weekly publication of the Jesuits of the United States of America.*

Points to Consider:

1. Why do public schools in the United States avoid religious education?
2. How are Canadian public schools managing to include religious education in the curriculum?
3. Could the Canadian experiments work in American public schools? Why or why not?

The Canadian cases do show that it is possible to find a place for the study of religion even in the public schools of the pluralistic society.

Like an intermittent fever, alarm about the nearly total neglect of religious education in public schools flares up periodically. It is currently at one of its peaks, and Education Secretary William J. Bennett has given this concern pungent expression.

Neglect of Religious Education

At the University of Missouri, during a lecture on "Religious Belief and the Constitutional Order," Mr. Bennett maintained that in the minds of the Republic's founders, "complete neutrality between particular religious beliefs can and should coexist with public acknowledgment of general religious values."

The Secretary argued that it should still be possible to give religion respect and public encouragement while scrupulously avoiding sectarianism or intolerance. It troubles him, therefore, to see that public schools, instead of trying to maintain "the delicate balance between religious faith and political tolerance," have practically banished religion altogether.

For extreme examples of this de facto secularism, Mr. Bennett drew upon a study made by New York University Professor Paul C. Vitz who found that most public school textbooks, probably out of fear of controversy, "go to extraordinary lengths to avoid any references to religion." Nor is this just a conservative conclusion. Two organizations that rarely agree with Secretary Bennett, Americans United for the Separation of Church and State along with People for the American Way, the lobby founded by television producer Norman Lear, concede that textbooks ignore the role religion has played in American history.

Canadian Experiments

In the United States, anticipation of trouble with the First Amendment has discouraged efforts to find constitutionally acceptable ways for public schools to make a little room for religious education. Interested parents and teachers can, however, pick up useful hints from the Canadian experiments described by Donald J. Weeren in *Educating Religiously in the Multi-Faith School,* a paperback just published by Detselig Enterprises in Calgary, Alberta.

In this slender but highly instructive book, Dr. Weeren, an associate professor of education at St. Mary's University in Halifax, provides a number of case studies that show how Canadian public schools with religiously heterogeneous faculties and student bodies manage to help

124

young people understand and appreciate their own religious faith and
that of others.

In Ontario, where province regulations call for opening or closing the
school day with religious exercises, the Toronto School Board has
worked up an anthology of readings and prayers that reflect the city's
pluralism by using not only the customary Christian materials but also
inspirational passages from a half-dozen other sources, including Hin-
duism and secular humanism. In Nova Scotia, an elective course in
biblical literature has been introduced into the regular curriculum of
a senior high school. In British Columbia, a unit on world religions is
part of the social studies course in a junior high school. Following the
British example, the publicly supported schools of Newfoundland and
Labrador have made religious instruction part of the regular curriculum
in each grade, but students are exempted at their parents' request. A
school in Halifax has set up what might be called a "released time"
program in which optional religion classes are taught by volunteers from
various churches during school hours and on school premises.

Could It Work in America?

Most of these experiments cannot be exactly reproduced in the
United States, where the relationship between religion and education
is far less constructive and flexible than it is in Canada, a nation whose
two most populous provinces, Ontario and Quebec, furnish tax support for denominational elementary and secondary schools. The Canadian cases that Dr. Weeren analyzes with persuasive detail do show,
however, that it is possible to find a place for the study of religion even
in the public schools of the pluralistic society.

Of course, not every one of those Canadian models could survive
here. U.S. conservatives, for instance, would be appalled by that Toronto

Cartoon by Bill Plympton. Reprinted with permission.

program whose rotated readings include snippets from Islam and ethical culture. But a released-time program taught in public school classrooms during the regular school day might work quite well. It cannot be tested, however, unless the U.S. Supreme Court reverses its 1948 McCollum decision. Such a reversal is unlikely, but not inconceivable. Some future court might decide that released time of this sort does not offend the Constitution because the Constitution, as Mr. Bennett remarked last month, "was written not only to protect our legal rights but also to express our common values."

WHAT IS EDITORIAL BIAS?

This activity may be used as an individualized study guide for students in libraries and resource centers or as a discussion catalyst in small group and classroom discussions.

The capacity to recognize an author's point of view is an essential reading skill. The skill to read with insight and understanding involves the ability to detect different kinds of opinions or bias. Sex bias, race bias, ethnocentric bias, political bias, and religious bias are five basic kinds of opinions expressed in editorials and all literature that attempts to persuade. They are briefly defined below.

---

5 Kinds of Editorial Opinion or Bias

SEX BIAS—The expression of dislike for and/or feeling of superiority over a person because of gender or sexual preference

RACE BIAS—The expression of dislike for and/or feeling of superiority over a racial group

ETHNOCENTRIC BIAS—The expression of a belief that one's own group, race, religion, culture, or nation is superior. Ethnocentric persons judge others by their own standards and values.

POLITICAL BIAS—The expression of political opinions and attitudes about domestic or foreign affairs

RELIGIOUS BIAS—The expression of a religious belief or attitude

---

Guidelines

1. From the readings in chapter three, locate five sentences that provide examples of editorial opinion or bias.

127

2. Write down each of the above sentences and determine what kind of bias each sentence represents. Is it *sex bias, race bias, ethnocentric bias, political bias, or religious bias?*

3. Make up one sentence statements that would be an example of each of the following: *sex bias, race bias, ethnocentric bias, political bias, and religious bias.*

4. See if you can locate five sentences that are factual statements from the readings in chapter three.

CHAPTER 4

RELIGION AND PUBLIC POLICY

RELIGION AND PUBLIC POLICY

WHEN RELIGION AND POLITICS SHOULD NOT MIX

Mark Amstutz

The following article, by Dr. Mark Amstutz, appeared in The Presbyterian Layman, *a conservative publication of the Presbyterian Lay Committee. The Committee is a nonprofit organization within the Presbyterian Church (USA).*

Points to Consider:

1. Describe the limitations of denominational resolutions.
2. Why was the U.S. Catholic Bishops' letter on the nuclear arms race so influential?
3. Summarize the author's principles for dealing with domestic and international politics.
4. Do you think denominational resolutions on domestic and international political concerns are beneficial to the mission of the church? Why or why not?

Mark Amstutz, "The Church and Public Policy," *The Presbyterian Layman,* January/February 1988, p. 10.

Mainline churches would strengthen their ministry immeasurably if they placed greater emphasis on their responsibility as teachers of biblical and moral principles and de-emphasized their advocacy of particular public policy alternatives.

Most mainline Protestant churches regularly pass denominational resolutions on domestic and international political concerns. In 1984, for example, the General Assembly of the Presbyterian church adopted several foreign policy resolutions, the most extensive one dealing with Central America. The resolution, approved without debate, stated that U.S. foreign policy toward the region was dominated by the "perceived threat of an expanding Soviet influence" and then went on to urge that the United States should halt its intervention in Nicaragua, pressure the government of El Salvador to prosecute and punish death squads, and stop foreign aid until the government reaches a negotiated settlement with opposition groups. A year later the 197th General Assembly adopted a similar resolution condemning U.S. Central American foreign policy, and called on President Reagan to repeal the executive order establishing a trade embargo against Nicaragua. The resolution also encouraged the "sanctuary" movement, commending congregations which had declared themselves as sanctuary communities and calling on other churches to do so.

Are resolutions such as these an important part of the redemptive witness of the church? Are they beneficial to the body politic? Do they contribute to the development of a moral public policy? I believe that the emphasis on resolutions and public policy advocacy is not only misguided but counterproductive to the central mission of the church.

Simplistic Solutions

Denominational resolutions have a number of serious limitations. First, they tend to be simplistic. While it may be tempting to offer simple moral verdicts on society's complex problems, offering simplistic, categorical judgments and solutions can be damaging to the credibility of the church.

Careless Biblical Analysis

Second, church resolutions are seldom based on careful biblical or moral analysis. The reason for this is that church pronouncements are not designed as teaching documents, but as instruments of public policy advocacy. Their aim is not to inform, but to mobilize public support and especially to influence the behavior of public officials. In their haste to address a vast array of public policy issues, churches seldom take the time to examine public policy problems dispassionately and bring biblical principles to bear on problems.

Seldom Representative

Third, resolutions are seldom representative of the organizations on whose behalf they allegedly speak. There are two reasons for this. First, the leadership of churches has historically been much more liberal politically than the rank and file. . . . Another reason is that the church, like any large organization, is dominated by special interests. As an organization increases in size, it tends to delegate its decision making to administrative heads. This pattern called the "iron law of oligarchy" by social scientists, is especially evident in political organizations, although church organizations are not immune from this problem. The result is that church leaders, who are often out of touch with the rank and file, devise proposals which do not reflect or represent views and convictions of the members on whose behalf they work.

Divisive Impact

A fourth weakness of denominational resolutions is that they are divisive. Politics is an arena of conflict and dispute. When churches adopt specific positions on complex issues in domestic and foreign affairs, they run the risk of creating bitter tension with the body of Christ. At the same time, they run the risk of becoming embroiled in the political conflicts of society, inevitably leading to some loss of moral authority. Alexis de Tocqueville, in his magisterial study *Democracy in America,* observes that "the church cannot share the temporal power of the state without being the object of a portion of that animosity which the latter excites." In carrying out its redemptive mission, the church needs to guard against overpolitization. If it does so, it will more likely be able to stress unity in essentials and diversity in unessentials.

132

Cartoon by David Seavey. Copyright 1984, *USA Today*. Reprinted with permission.

Failing to Teach

But the chief shortcoming of denominational resolutions is that they divert attention from the more important task of structuring the moral parameters of public policy debates. By focusing on resolutions and policy options, the church neglects its role in clarifying and applying moral principles to contemporary public policy issues. It thus fails to be a moral teacher. This is most regrettable, since the structuring of the moral parameters is one of the most important ways by which the church can bring its redemptive witness to bear in the political arena.

David McKenna has observed that the church has four important responsibilities: prayer, preaching, teaching, and fellowship. The church's role in the political arena derives from its teaching responsibilities. For example, as a teacher in foreign affairs, the church can help identify the fundamental moral interests of the nation and provide moral and biblical guidance on public policy debates. Since government officials are often guided by immediate, tangible national interests, the church can help identify the long-term moral interests of the nation. While security of a state is a legitimate concern, the church must prod the consciences of citizens by clarifying and articulating the moral basis of a nation's fundamental interests. Just as morality must help to illuminate, guide, and refine the conception of the national interest, the church must similarly help define legitimate national goals, as well as means to achieve them.

Biblical Principles

The second teaching responsibility of the church is to help frame the public policy debates by illuminating relevant biblical principles and major moral assumptions. Paul Ramsey, a distinguished ethics professor, has called attention to the limited but vital role of the Christian faith in public affairs: "The religious communities as such should be concerned with perspectives upon politics, with political doctrines, with the direction and structures of common life, not with specific directives. They should seek to clarify and keep wide open the legitimate options for choice, and thus nurture the moral and political ethics of the nation. Their task is not the determination of policy."

What is important to recognize is that the church's competency is not in domestic or international politics but in moral and biblical analysis. The church must do what it does best—bringing a Christian worldview to bear on public policy formation—and avoid doing what it does not do well—namely, devising specific policies in response to contemporary world problems. The first is the responsibility of church leaders; the second is the task of the government officials. As the noted British historian Herbert Butterfield once noted, "it isn't the function of churches to solve problems of diplomacy." The church does not have competency in nuclear weapons, international trade, or immigration policy. Ecclesiastical officials have less competency on these issues than professionally trained officials whose sole task concerns these issues. The competence of church officials lies not in the social sciences, but in biblical and moral discernment. The job of making public policy is entrusted to elected and appointed government officials. However tempting it may be to offer policy recommendations, religious organizations would be well advised to use caution in offering specific domestic or foreign policy advice. If the church is to be effective in public affairs, it must do what it has been called to do and what it does best—namely, to be the salt and light of the world.

Competence Needed

Let me suggest a number of principles which would make Christians more effective in their task of redeeming domestic and international politics. First, the church needs to address issues competently and dispassionately. One of the reasons why the U.S. Catholic Bishops' letter on the nuclear dilemma ("The Challenge of Peace") has been so influential is that the Bishops undertook their study with thoroughness, relying on expert testimony in various areas relevant to the moral dilemma of nuclear weapons. Whether or not one agrees with the policies advocated by the bishops, the careful preparation of this letter earned the Catholic bishops deep admiration and respect.

Humility Needed

Second, the church needs to carry out its task of moral teaching in the political domain with humility. Christians need to remember that all political choices bear the consequences of human fallenness. Because of the radical nature of sin, our understanding of issues will always bear the results of human finiteness. There can therefore be no single Christian policy on the dominant concerns within our country or the world. Realizing this should not lead to paralysis but to humble political activity.

Moral Teaching Needed

Third, the church should concentrate its influence on the illumination and application of principles to particular issues. Since moral authority tends to decline with the increasing specificity of policies advocated by groups, the church should concentrate its influence on teaching, rather than public policy advocacy. For example, some mainline churches have passed resolutions on South Africa, but the emphasis on economic sanctions found in some church statements seems ill advised. The churches would be more effective and faithful in their ministry if they de-emphasized their interest in tactics (e.g., economic sanctions) and addressed the existing unjust and immoral political and economic structures in that land.

Prudence Needed

Fourth, the church needs to emphasize the relevance of multiple ethical norms to contemporary political issues. There is no significant social or political problem in which only one ethical value or principle is relevant. Indeed, the great challenge in moral politics is to weigh the relative merits of competing moral norms. This is why prudence is an essential virtue for Christians involved in political redemption.

Finally, in carrying out its political redemptive ministry, the church should avoid the fallacy of dichotomous thinking—that is, viewing political alternatives in mutually exclusive categories. The error of this approach becomes particularly injurious when "either/or" thinking is applied to divisive issues in society—such as SDI, Central American foreign policy, tax policy, abortion, peacekeeping. It is important to recall that political debates are not between saints and sinners but among sinners.

Peter writes that Christians are "a chosen race, a royal priesthood, a holy nation." If the church is to be more effective in bearing witness to redemption, then it will have to carry out its responsibilities to the political domain with greater discrimination, discernment, and skill. Mainline Protestant churches, in particular, would strengthen their ministry immeasurably if they placed greater emphasis on their responsibility as teachers of biblical and moral principles and de-emphasized their advocacy of particular public policy alternatives.

WHEN CHURCH AND POLITICS
SHOULD MIX

Arthur Simon

This reading is excerpted from Christian Faith & Public Policy: No
Grounds for Divorce, *written by Arthur Simon. Mr. Simon wrote this
book in his capacity as executive director of Bread for the World, an
American, Christian citizens' movement working for better policy
responses to world hunger.*

Points to Consider:

1. Why does the author believe churches should take a stand on
   political issues of great moral importance?
2. How can local churches best address public policy issues?
3. Analyze the role of the pastor and other leaders in the local church
   with regard to inviting church members to participate in public policy
   concerns.
4. Explain why official church statements regarding public policy issues
   are often ignored.

Arthur Simon, *Christian Faith and Public Policy: No Grounds for Divorce*
(Grand Rapids, MI.: William B. Eerdmans Publishing Company, 1987),
pp. 66-81. Reprinted with permission of William B. Eerdmans Publishing
Company.

The church should not use the need to distance itself from partisan politics as an excuse to avoid speaking out on political issues of great moral importance.

In June 1982, a committee of Roman Catholic bishops, working on behalf of the National Conference of Catholic Bishops, released the first draft of an extensive report on the nuclear arms race. The report analyzed the main aspects of this issue, which it assessed in the light of Christian moral principles. The report immediately hit the front pages of newspapers, got coverage on television networks, and became the cover story of *Time, Newsweek,* and other magazines. Such media attention for a church's assessment of a public policy issue was unprecedented. Coming at a time when the "new Religious Right" had emerged as a major participant in the national political arena, the report underscored the involvement of churches in public affairs. In combination, these developments raised an important question to a new level of visibility: What is the proper role of the churches with regard to the affairs of government?. . .

Religion and Life: No Grounds for Divorce

I want to stress the importance of distinguishing between the separation of church and state, and the separation of religion and life. The latter puts much of life outside the boundary of faith, contradicting the reality that Jesus Christ is Lord of our entire life. The distinction applies to the church as well as to the individual, though one often hears clergy and laity alike suggest that the church has no business dealing with policy issues.

"The church's job is to preach the gospel, not get involved in politics," it is said—and there is a sense in which this pronouncement is valid. It is a mistake for churches to get mired in *partisan* politics. It is the essence of the church's mission and ministry to preach, teach, and celebrate God's work of redeeming us through Jesus Christ. However, such preaching and celebration cannot occur in a vacuum. They occur in the context of real life and real problems, both individual and social. Thus proclaiming and celebrating the gospel faithfully means doing so specifically—for example, in relation to the family. Not the family as an abstraction, but the real family that one belongs to—your family or my family—composed of people with warts, wrinkles, and clay feet, with joys and heartaches, growing pains and needs. Through our families God has placed most of us in a position of special responsibility toward some very precious people. Because our understanding and our capacity to respond are limited, we need to do all that we can to help one another strengthen our family relationships so that our hopes for one another and the steps we take to realize these hopes partake more fully of God's intention for us. If someone were to tell us that it is the church's job to preach the gospel and not to get involved in family life, we would instinctively protest that the church, if it is to proclaim and live the gospel faithfully, must necessarily be involved in matters of family life and cannot possibly remove so important an area of life from its concern. If Jesus has no place in my family concerns, then he is not truly my Lord and Savior.

For much the same reason, the church cannot duck public issues of exceptional importance that profoundly affect the lives of others. That leaves open the question of *how* it should respond. There are wise ways and foolish ways, of course. But the church does not faithfully respond to the biblical witness regarding the injustice of hunger, for example, unless it pays attention to policy decisions that affect the hungry. More broadly cast, the church should not use the need to distance itself from partisan politics as an excuse to avoid speaking out on political issues of great moral importance. . . .

In reality there is no such thing as "not getting involved" or never taking a stand on critical moral issues, because not taking a stand *is* taking a stand in support of the status quo or the direction in which things may be moving. The classic example of this is provided by the church in Germany during the rise of Hitler. There were notable and courageous exceptions, to be sure, but for the most part, pastors, priests, and laypeople said the church should stick to preaching the gospel and stay away from politics. It was a comfortable, safe response. But in retrospect it is clear that far from being uninvolved in politics, the church was deeply mired in it, for the church's neutrality was understood as consent to the Nazi program. The church's neutrality was an illusion, a tragic misjudgment. . . .

139

Cartoon by David Seavey. Copyright 1988, *USA Today*. Reprinted with permission.

Local Churches and Policy Issues

When we ask how a local church can best address public policy issues, the answer first of all is that the church's essential task is not that of addressing public policy issues but the ministry of the gospel or, put differently, the carrying out of the Great Commission of Jesus. That said, it must immediately be added that the ministry of the gospel, this commission to make disciples, has as a major purpose the calling and equipping of people in Christ for a life of service. It is in this connection that the local church should see its public policy role. How can its members be equipped for service to others? That service, if fully embraced, includes the offering of our citizenship to God for the benefit of others, and part of Christian citizenship is the advocating of policies that will enhance human life.

The local church can do this in ways that the national church body cannot, because the local church is where the people are. Quintessentially, the church is the local communion of believers, not a national institution. It is here that God's people gather to pray, praise, and nourish one another in the life of faith. And so here, most of all, is where the opportunity lies for integrating public policy concerns into a full expression of the gospel. Either that happens in the local congregation, or it probably does not happen at all.

The Sunday worship (service, mass) is only the first and most important of ways in which a local church can develop its commitment and understanding with regard to Christ and the world. The development of such commitment will embrace much more than public policy issues. These should be seen in the larger context of citizenship and the still larger context of one's whole life as an offering to God. Participating in the local PTA, serving on the local school board, taking part in a neighborhood improvement campaign, or becoming active in the local precinct of one's political party—these are among the many ways in which people can get involved, for good reasons or bad, in public affairs. Christians should be encouraged to think about such involvement as a specifically Christian ministry and given opportunity to discuss such service with fellow believers. This can be done in a way that does not divide people but helps them understand their Christian calling. Such a context provides a training ground and preparation for work on policy issues as well.

The role of church leaders, especially that of the pastor, deserves special comment. In my view, the pastor should not see himself or herself as a policy expert commissioned to deliver answers from the pulpit—a top-down approach that is inappropriate and seldom effective, as well as unfair to both the pastor and the congregation. This approach is apt to be divisive because people will see themselves pressed to embrace the pastor's political preferences, which, they may suspect, do not spring from divine revelation. A dose of well-founded humility on these matters will be greatly appreciated. . . .

The pastor and other leaders in the local church do well to guard against moralism. By moralism I mean exhortations to do good ("Write your member of Congress about famine in Africa") that are not grounded in God's saving love and therefore do not sound like an opportunity to love and serve God in return. The desired action should be presented as an invitation to respond to the gospel and human need. The word "invitation" is crucial, because the intention should not be to pressure people into action or to make them feel like moral lepers if they do not respond in a certain way, but to let them experience the joy of serving others.

In addition, it is unfair to ask people to take action for which they do not feel sufficiently prepared. Not everyone is at the same level of preparation or can be expected to arrive at the same conclusion regarding the best course of action. So it is wise if, within the context of a grace-oriented invitation (as opposed to a law-oriented exhortation), the pastor gives members of the congregation the time and opportunity to consider an issue together.

The Sunday worship (service, mass) is the heart of the congregation's life as a community of believers, so what happens here affects everything else. The biblical lessons or texts used in most churches provide a wide range of opportunities—too seldom utilized—to bring various issues to the congregation's attention. The preaching, the prayers, and even the singing can and should reflect a ministry to the world—but not in a way that makes people feel badgered and certainly not in a way that detracts from the centrality of God's love in Christ. Attention to our earthly citizenship should not make us feel that our heavenly citizenship is being slighted. The latter reality should, in fact, inform and motivate us regarding the former. . . .

National Church Bodies and Policy Issues

There is a widespread wariness in local congregations about the role of national church bodies in relation to public policy issues. One reason for such wariness is the feeling of many that "the church should stick to religion"—a feeling that is at least partly misguided. Another reason is that church members who express their views are sometimes challenged, and that seldom induces comfort. Those challenged often feel that their views have not been taken into account by leaders who have imposed their own flawed conclusions. This feeling is also partly misguided because there are often sound theological reasons for challenging views in the pews. All of this said, the uneasiness regarding the role of national church bodies in relation to policy issues, as well as the response to that uneasiness, should be considered from this standpoint: that the ministry of the church, including its ministry in the public policy arena, belongs to all of the people of God.

Church leaders have a special opportunity to guide the church in addressing policy issues; they should bear in mind that their task is ultimately to help equip Christians in the local congregations for effective service. However, church members do not have to wait passively for others in the church to speak for them. The principle that applies in government applies in the church as well: Those willing to take part in considering an issue and expressing views on it will have an influence far greater than their numbers simply because most other people do not bother to get involved in policy issues.

Selection of Issues

·Since church bodies cannot address every policy issue that comes along, the selection of issues is important. As a rule, the fewer issues they address, the more they may be able to focus well and effective-ly. . . .

Official Statements

One of the most common ways in which national church bodies address public policy issues is through official statements. These may be issued by a council of bishops, a church commission, or a group of delegates at a national church convention. They may come from a wider national or international body of Christians representing one or many denominations. Or they may come from a single authority, such as the pope, who from time to time writes encyclicals (letters to the church) on social and moral issues.

Issuing statements is one thing. Getting people to consider and act on them is quite another. With notable exceptions, official statements are widely ignored. They may still have considerable importance, perhaps influencing people at various levels of leadership, but usually they do not get attention within local congregations because such statements are seldom discussed there. If this is true of the response of local churches to statements from national church bodies, it is even more true of the response of Protestants to reports or resolutions coming from associations that represent many church bodies or from a world-wide denominational gathering. My impression is that Christians in local churches tend to think that their own denominational leadership is none too close to them, and that the larger national and international entities to which their denomination belongs are still further removed, so they do not readily identify with these groups. In addition, if my sense of the situation is correct, most church members are not all that interested in public policy issues, and many who are tend to think that church groups and church leaders possess no better understanding of such issues than they do. Whatever the reasons, official church statements are not automatic attention-getters.

What is the "target group" for such statements? The general public may sometimes be perceived as the audience, but it pays little attention—though there are exceptions to this rule. Even if statements occasionally get media coverage, they are quickly forgotten by most of the public. Are public officials the intended audience? Members of Congress seldom hold their breath waiting to see what the Presbyterians or the Baptists or any other denomination has to say about an issue, although there may be scattered interest. No, the people for whom such statements are primarily intended are the members of the religious body that issues the statements. *The key question, therefore, is how effectively does a statement invite members of local churches to think about an issue, discuss it, and take subsequent action?* And if the action is to influence a policy decision, then we are back to the basic matters of citizenship and advocacy. . . .

143

There is no perfect process that ought always to be followed in developing official statements, but church members need to be drawn into the process, for their ministry, their Christian service, is paramount. . . .

I am giving more attention to the question of official statements than to other ways in which national church bodies take up public policy issues. This is misleading in a way, but I choose this emphasis because I think there is confusion regarding the purpose of such statements, a tendency to think of them as ends in themselves rather than as means of engaging Christians in ministry.

18

RELIGION AND PUBLIC POLICY

HOW THE RELIGIOUS RIGHT ABUSES RELIGION

Arland Jacobsen

Arland Jacobsen wrote the following article in his capacity as director of the CHARIS Ecumenical Center at Concordia College in Moorhead, Minnesota. The article appeared in the Star Tribune, *a newspaper of Minneapolis/St. Paul, Minnesota.*

Points to Consider:

1. Define "fundamentalist."
2. Why are fundamentalists angry?
3. How do fundamentalists plan to solve the problem of disorder?
4. In what ways does the Religious Right abuse religion?

Arland Jacobsen, "The Angry Fundamentalist's Quest to Capture a City for Christ," *Star Tribune*, August 17, 1987. Reprinted by permission of the *Star Tribune, Newspaper of the Twin Cities.*

The gospel is not so much a word of comfort and liberation as a weapon used to do battle against a world that the fundamentalist fears.

Jerry Falwell's a fundamentalist. Billy Graham is an evangelical. Jim Bakker and Pat Robertson are pentecostals. These well-known evangelists often sound, look, and talk alike. How can you tell who's who?

"A fundamentalist is an evangelical who is angry about something," says Duke University historian George Marsden in a Sept. 2, 1985, *Time* magazine article. While different fundamentalist groups display varying degrees of militancy, that single characteristic—anger—most sets fundamentalists apart from evangelicals and other religious groups.

Why are They Angry?

What are fundamentalists angry about? Mostly—it seems—disorder, confusion, uncertainty, compromise, moral relativism, and weakness.

To the fundamentalist, the world seems to be floundering in chaos. He or she is angry at the world and believes God is, too. Provoking the fundamentalist's anger are new ideas, values, standards; sexually explicit rock music; political and world affairs gone out of control; and other changes that have turned the fundamentalists' familiar world topsy-turvy.

"This isn't how we remember the world being," cry the fundamentalists. Home, school, family, church—everything seems to have fallen into disorder.

Fundamentalists offer to the world a nostalgic vision of order—of moral absolutes, of religious certainty, of rigid conformity to certain favorite standards. To submit to this magnificently ordered world is called "being born again." This, for fundamentalists, is not simply an emotional experience but an act of the will—an act of submission. This is why powerful preachers play such a dominant role in fundamentalism.

The solution to the great problem of disorder is to submit to authorities who convey a sense of being in control, of having the right answers. Fundamentalist history, therefore, is largely one of powerful personalities; the source of this strong streak of authoritarianism is that tremendous need for order.

Bringing Order Through Action

But how is this vision of order to be realized in a world filled with confusion and compromise? At one time the main technique was separation from the world. A fiercely protected enclave of order would be carved out of the messy world. But moderate fundamentalists such as

146

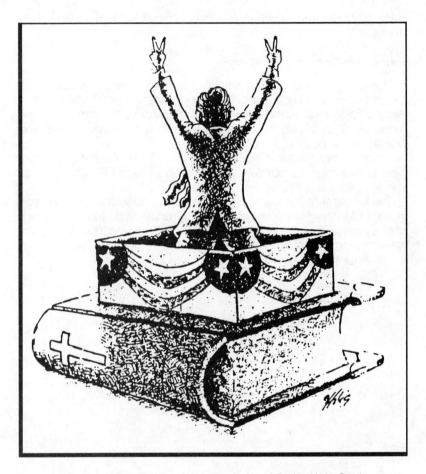

Illustration by Dan Hubig. Reprinted with permission of Pacific News Service.

Jerry Falwell demonstrate their militancy not so much by separation as by trying to bring order to the world through action.

One kind of action is political: mobilizing the votes of the righteous; attacking opponents; leading demonstrations against all manner of evil, from pornography to abortion. But there is another way to bring order to the world—what Jerry Falwell calls "super aggressive evangelism." In "The Complete Book of Church Growth," Falwell writes, "It is my conviction that every local church should attempt to capture its city for Christ."

What would it mean to "capture a city for Christ?" It would mean to impose on that city the values and beliefs of the fundamentalists. In short, it would take the unruly, confused world and impose order

147

upon it. Their order. That, in essence, is what fundamentalism is all about.

Using the Gospel as a Weapon

The Gospel is not so much a word of comfort and liberation as a weapon used to do battle against a world that the fundamentalist fears. As one Falwell associate, Elmer Towns, explained, "Evangelism is the force used to transform an alien world into a recognizable and homogenous body of born-again saints."

Unfortunately, the belief that the world is in chaos and that order must be imposed upon it produces intolerance and zealotry. Fundamentalists are anti-pluralistic and anti-ecumenical.

The fundamentalist spirit appears to be superpatriotic, but it is utterly out of touch with the American liberal democratic tradition, which allows people of every kind to live together. Fundamentalism does not reflect the true spirit of Christianity. Christianity does not recoil in horror at what is new or different.

19 RELIGION AND PUBLIC POLICY

HOW THE RELIGIOUS LEFT ABUSES RELIGION

Elliot Rothenberg

Elliot Rothenberg wrote the following article in his capacity as president of the North Star Legal Foundation. The views expressed in this reading are his own. The article appeared in the Minneapolis Star and Tribune.

Points to Consider:

1. In what ways has the religious left abused religion?
2. Examine the mixing of religion and politics and discuss the effects one has upon the other.
3. Describe the role of clergymen in speaking out on political issues.
4. Compare and contrast the left- and right-wing abuses of religion.

Elliot Rothenberg, "Ignoring the Left's Abuse of Religion," *Minneapolis Star and Tribune,* October 4, 1984. Reprinted by permission of *Star Tribune, Newspaper of the Twin Cities.*

To harp on arguable religious intolerance of the right while ignoring blatant appeals to religious bigotry by the left is to engage in hypocrisy.

Liberal politicians and writers condemn the Reagan campaign and certain clergymen for allegedly introducing religion into politics and threatening the separation of church and state. They have failed to acknowledge, however, that the issue is a double-edged sword.

Several matters involved in the current controversy—such as abortion, school prayer, and tuition tax credits for parochial schools—are subjects of legitimate concern. In a more general sense, the confounding of religion and politics is alarming to those who subscribe to differing religious views.

Left-Wing Abuse of Religion

Nevertheless, the moral posturing of much of the commentary has been highly selective. The use and abuse of religious authority to advance political positions is not limited to the right.

The World Council of Churches has become notorious for its funding of leftist regimes and movements, all in disregard of the viewpoints of its members. Area churches and synagogues have aided nuclear-freeze and similar groups. The political programs of liberal clerics have characteristics of a religious and moral crusade, along with claims of Biblical inspiration and support comparable to those of the Moral Majority.

Neither is moral and religious intolerance for opposing opinions limited to the Religious Right. The same scholars who denounce bishops for publicizing their positions on abortion condone and even encourage clergy and churches to support the nuclear freeze movement and Marxist terrorists in Central America and elsewhere.

Mixing Religion and Politics

Those ostensibly concerned with religious freedom remained silent about 1984's most frightening example of mixing religion and politics— the strident anti-Semitism of the Jesse Jackson-Louis Farrakhan presidential campaign.

Almost as appalling as the outbursts of Jackson and Farrakhan was the abdication of moral responsibility by the national Democratic Party in the face of what was very likely the most bigoted campaign ever run by a serious candidate for the presidential nomination of a major party.

Fundamental decency demanded a forthright and unambiguous renouncement by Jackson's party of his campaign's instigation of religious hatred. However, the Democratic national convention refused even to consider a resolution condemning religious bigotry in general and anti-

Cartoon by Web Bryant. Copyright 1985, *USA Today*. Reprinted with permission.

Semitism in particular. So did the Democratic National Committee. Finally, and only after the Republican convention highlighted the issue, a Democratic executive committee approved a similar resolution by a telephone poll.

Although there have been a few honorable exceptions, such as *The New Republic* magazine, most of the recent writing on religion and politics has reflected a barely-disguised bias.

Engaging in Hypocrisy

To assert that the archbishop of New York may not speak out on abortion but does have the moral authority to advocate nuclear disarmament is to reduce an already sanctimonious argument to the level of caricature. To harp on arguable religious intolerance of the right while ignoring blatant appeals to religious bigotry by the left is to engage in hypocrisy.

Ironically, the abuses of religion in politics by both politicians and religious figures, on the left as well as on the right, are even more pervasive than indicated in the recent writings on the subject, which have focused on only one side's activities. Geraldine Ferraro's charge that President Reagan "is not a good Christian" is the obverse of Reagan's own comments about the relation of religion and politics.

Religious leaders of the left and the right have used spiritual authority to push political programs. The confusion of politics and religion has had harmful effects for religion and for the political process. All should unite in condemning appeals to religious bigotry.

Clergymen of all religions and of whatever political ideology have the right to speak out as individuals on political issues just like everyone else. They ought not, however, purport to have divine guidance for their political pronouncements.

God should not be blamed for the mistakes of mortals.

20 RELIGION AND PUBLIC POLICY

RELIGION AND POLITICS: POINTS AND COUNTERPOINTS

The Christian Voice vs. Americans for Religious Liberty

The Christian Voice was founded by the Reverend Robert G. Grant and a number of leading Christian spokesmen in 1978. The Christian Voice was the nation's first conservative, evangelical Christian lobbying effort—and today, it is the largest.

Americans for Religious Liberty is a nonprofit public interest educational organization dedicated to preserving the American tradition of religious, intellectual, and personal freedom in a secular democratic state.

Points to Consider:

1. Describe the National Opinion Survey Ballot. How does the Christian Voice plan to use it?
2. What is the Christian Voice Report Card? Summarize its effect on American politics.
3. According to Americans for Religious Liberty, what specific actions are Religious Right groups taking to impose their agenda on the country?
4. Compare and contrast the Christian Voice's and the Americans for Religious Liberty's appeals for monetary contributions.

The Point is reprinted from a 1985 public letter written by one of the Christian Voice's founders, Rev. Robert G. Grant. The Counterpoint is reprinted from a 1987 public letter written by Isaac Asimov, a member of the Americans for Religious Liberty's National Advisory Board.

THE POINT—
by The Christian Voice

Dear Christian Friend,

Ten U.S. Senators and Congressmen confided to me that the *reason we are losing America* is because Christians like you and I have never had a *politically effective* voice in Washington, D.C.

This is why I need to have your response to the important moral questions on the enclosed National Opinion Survey Ballot *before I next meet with your Senators and Congressmen.*

By *doing nothing,* we Christians have allowed the liberals and "moderates" in Washington to put God's legislation on the back burner and keep pushing the socialist-atheist agenda.

That's why Congress is still pushing such things as:

- A national "Gay Rights Law" that will force Christian schools and family businesses to hire homosexuals—including those with AIDS.

- Banning all prayer in public schools.

- Liberal pornography and child molesting laws.

- IRS attempts to close down private Christian schools by revoking their tax-exempt status.

- Taxpayer-paid "abortion-on-demand" for any woman who wants one.

- Dismantling our national defenses.

- Increased government spending for wasteful welfare and other Big Government schemes.

Well, I can tell you that's not what I voted for and I don't think you voted for these outrages either!

But I can't *prove that* to your Senators and Congressmen unless you help me by filling out the National Opinion Survey Ballot.

If pressure-group politics is the only way to get anything done, then we Christians absolutely *have to be the biggest and strongest "pressure group"* around.

This is why I, with a number of leading Christian spokesmen, started Christian Voice (CV) back in 1978. CV was the nation's *first* conservative, evangelical Christian lobbying effort on Capitol Hill in Washington, D.C.

Sixty-five Senators and Congressmen along with distinguished leaders from other national organizations have joined CV's Advisory Committee. We have already received credit for winning many major battles in Congress.

Even the liberal news media and political pollsters were forced to admit that our efforts were crucial in educating millions of Christians who defeated 38 *liberal Senators and Congressmen in 1980 and 1984.*

A NEW POWERFUL FORCE

"Millions of Christians appear to be coming together to form a new powerful force. In the Vanguard is Christian Voice. . .Christian Voice is being heard in Washington, D.C., loud and clear!"

Excerpted from a special "60 Minutes" segment about Christian Voice

For the *first time in history* millions of Christians were able to see how their Congressmen voted on 14 key moral issues. . .like abortion, homosexuality, pornography, communism, etc. That's why Christian Voice is famous for our Report Cards on Congress.

And that's why the *liberals hate us.* In 1980 Jimmy Carter attacked us in a national TV speech; in 1984 Walter Mondale did the same. The liberals have sworn to destroy our Report Cards. Why?

The book *God's Bullies,* written as a vicious attack on us, had to admit after interviewing hundreds of defeated candidates: "The most despised—that is effective—device used by Christian Voice is its Report Card—distributed with devastating impact each year to millions of Christians."

You and I have to convince our elected representatives that homosexuals and atheists aren't the only ones who have "rights." We have rights, too! But they're being *taken away from us* one by one—and we're tired of it. WE WANT OUR COUNTRY BACK!

It's *OUR money* the government is squandering *every day* on useless and immoral programs, including "homosexual rights" and taxpayer-paid abortions.

It's in OUR schools that they've banned religion; government has replaced God with sex, drugs, illiteracy, and rampant violence. We want our SCHOOLS back!

The government is trampling all over OUR sacred and cherished Christian beliefs. . . .and we're sick of it!

WE WANT OUR COUNTRY BACK—the way it was *before* God was banned from the classroom—*before* the vilest pornography was allowed to be put on the magazine shelf in every corner drugstore and *before* the liberals made our streets safe for rapists and muggers, but not for God-fearing people.

We will fight with every ounce of our strength to restore the traditional American Christian values in Washington, but it's a *tough, uphill fight.*

It's going to be a lot harder than I ever imagined it would be but I know God will give us the power we need to win the fight.

I am writing to you today to ask *your help.* I am praying that God will put it in your heart to open your checkbook, and send the most

155

generous free-will gift you can afford to join your voice with ours to help Christian Voice turn the U.S. Congress, and the United States of America, back to God.

With your help, and with God's help, we will get the moral legislation off the back burner and onto the law books.

We *will* have prayer restored in our public schools. We *will* defeat laws forcing us to allow homosexuals access to our children and our tax dollars.

We *will* outlaw child pornographers, rapists, and child molesters—and see they stay in prison *without* parole! We *will* restore our national defense and economy to the strength they once enjoyed.

And we *will* restore the traditional American, Christian values and return America to the ways of the Lord, and once again secure the blessings and protection from our enemies as He has done in the past.

But to do all that, I need your help *today.*

The hard facts of life are that it costs a lot of money to run an effective, hard-hitting Christian lobby in Washington, D.C. and to keep *you* informed every month.

It costs money to publicize the Christian position on the moral issues to tens of millions of Christians so that we can motivate them to pressure their Senators and Congressmen. We are the *only ones* doing this crucial task! We spent over one million dollars last year on T.V., radio, and printing just to distribute our nation-changing Report Cards!

And the only source of funds we have is generous free-will gifts from concerned Christians like you.

I am calling you now to take a quiet moment to ask the Lord in prayer if it's His will that you should send a gift to Christian Voice today. Does He want you to be *His* instrument today, to send desperately-needed financial help to His ministry on Capitol Hill in Washington, D.C.?

And if the Lord does put it in your heart to send a check to Christian Voice, then I know you'll want to send the largest gift you can afford.

Unlike many organizations, you will see that we have a very small administrative overhead—I will send you, at your request, a copy of our financial report so you can see for yourself how effective we are with your hard-earned dollars!

If you can afford $25, $50, or $100, then I hope you will send that much. But if $10 or $15 is the most you can send today, we need it desperately and will be very grateful.

I know it's His will that Christian Voice is working to be the *Christian conscience of the U.S. Congress.* I know it's His will that your Senators and Congressmen be reminded daily of their responsibility to protect America's traditional Christian values.

It is His will that guided me to write this urgent appeal for help to you today. I don't think He would have led me to write to you if He didn't mean for you to join in this vitally important work.

So please ask *Him* about Christian Voice, and then send me your most generous free-will gift today.

In His Name,

Rev. Robert G. Grant, Ph.D.

P.S. I know you get so many appeals for help. Sometimes it's hard to know who's really *doing the most effective* job with your dollars! Please read carefully the statement from one of the top 10 leaders of the U.S. Senate—*Phil Gramm* of Texas.

"The Christian Voice 'Report Card' you distributed educated our people about the real issues of the 1984 campaign and were key to our victory. America needs Christian Voice."

Hon. Phil Gramm
U.S. Senator

NATIONAL OPINION SURVEY ON MORALITY ISSUES

Please take a few moments to give us your response to these four important questions.

Confidential: Only the percentage results of this survey will ever be released to U.S. Senators and Congressmen and the news media.

1) Do you want Congress to defeat a proposed federal law that would require schools, both public and private, to hire practicing homosexuals as teachers?

   ☐ Yes   ☐ No   ☐ Undecided

2) Do you want Congress to overturn the Supreme Court ruling that banned all prayer in America's public schools?

   ☐ Yes   ☐ No   ☐ Undecided

3) Do you want Congress to pass a constitutional amendment outlawing the killing of unborn babies through abortion?

   ☐ Yes   ☐ No   ☐ Undecided

4) Do you want Congress to end attempts by the Internal Revenue Service to destroy the Christian school movement by revoking the tax exempt status of private Christian schools?

   ☐ Yes   ☐ No   ☐ Undecided

The Christian Voice's National Opinion Survey Ballot.

THE COUNTERPOINT—
by Americans for Religious Liberty

Dear Friend,

Most Americans thought it was settled.

Our personal, intellectual, and religious freedom—we had come to take for granted—was guaranteed by the principle of separation of church and state in the Constitution and by other provisions of the Bill of Rights. Our rights were secure, we thought, and the courts would always stand behind them.

What we didn't count on was the rise in recent years of powerful Radical Right groups with names like "Moral Majority" and "Christian Voice." Two of the most important Radical Right leaders, Moral Majority's Jerry Falwell and the 700 Club's Pat Robertson, control media empires worth over a *quarter billion dollars* annually and influence many millions of Americans with their incessant propaganda.

New Religious Right leaders and groups too numerous even to list have joined with other sectarian special interests and opportunistic politicians to impose a frightening agenda on our country. Through massive media and direct mail campaigns, pressures in and on Congress, state legislatures and school boards, and gross misuse of religious impulses, they are working to—

- Impose government regimented group prayer on all students in our public schools

- Encourage fundamentalist proselytizing in public schools under the "equal access" legislation passed by Congress in 1984

- Downgrade science teaching in public schools in favor of the pseudoscientific, fundamentalist doctrine of "creationism"

- Force all taxpayers to support sectarian private schools (which provide sectarian indoctrination and proactive religious, ideological, and other forms of discrimination) through vouchers and tuition tax credits

- Deny women with problem pregnancies the constitutional right to choose safe, legal abortions

- Weaken the right to read and the right to know by censoring textbooks, libraries, and school curricula

- Apply religious litmus tests for federal judges

- Deny federal courts jurisdiction over important First Amendment cases

Illustration reprinted with permission of Americans for Religious Liberty.

- Call a national constitutional convention (the first since 1787) to graft their radical agenda onto the Constitution itself

What many Americans have yet to grasp is that our courts may not be able to save the situation. If *just one* of the Court's strong supporters of the First Amendment retires (and four are older than Ronald Reagan), it is likely that the Supreme Court will shift dramatically to the Moral Majority side.

Jerry Falwell has boasted that the Radical Right has developed a voting bloc large enough to "redirect" the country's future. TV evangelist and faith healer Pat Robertson is making noises like a 1988 presidential candidate.

Most Americans reject the Radical Right agenda, but they are not adequately organized to stop the moral majoritarian juggernaut.

But all is not lost. We the people can make the crucial difference. We can and *will* determine, by action or inaction, whether our country progresses toward ever greater freedom or turns the calendar back to an intolerant, obscurantist Dark Age. Defenders of freedom and church-state separation have won impressive victories in the courts, in Congress, in state legislatures, and in referendum elections on school prayer, creationism, abortion rights, tax aid for sectarian schools, freedom of expression, etc. Voices of reason, though usually outspent and outorganized, won anyway.

We—you and I and other Americans who care about our basic freedoms—can, MUST concentrate and multiply our efforts. One very good way to do that is through AMERICANS FOR RELIGIOUS LIBERTY, on whose National Advisory Board I am pleased to serve.

Americans for Religious Liberty (ARL) is a nationwide, nonprofit, educational organization open to all who share its deep commitment to the American ideals of pluralism and church-state separation. Through its publications, speakers bureau, coast-to-coast media appearances, research, testimony before Congress, litigation activity, coalition building, and grass roots organizing, ARL is making an increasingly important difference.

I urge you to do your part *today* by sending ARL a check—for a basic membership or for whatever amount you think our liberties are worth. Every donation, large or small, really counts. Donations are tax-deductible. All donor/members receive the informative ARL newsletter, *Voice of Reason.*

Yours for freedom,

Isaac Asimov
National Advisory Board
Americans for Religious Liberty

INTERPRETING
EDITORIAL CARTOONS

This activity may be used as an individualized study guide for students in libraries and resource centers or as a discussion catalyst in small group and classroom discussions.

Although cartoons are usually humorous, the main intent of most political cartoonists is not to entertain. Cartoons express serious social comment about important issues. Using graphic and visual arts, the cartoonist expresses opinions and attitudes. By employing an entertaining and often light-hearted visual format, cartoonists may have as much or more impact on national and world issues as editorial and syndicated columnists.

Points to Consider:

1. Examine the cartoon in this activity (see next page).

2. How would you describe the message of this cartoon? Try to describe the message in one to three sentences.

3. Do you agree with the message? Why or why not?

4. Does the cartoon support the author's point of view in any of the readings in this book? If the answer is yes, be specific about which reading or readings and why.

Cartoon by Joel Kauffman. Reprinted with permission from Joel Kauffmann and *Presbyterian Survey.*

BIBLIOGRAPHY

I. Reference materials on Martin Luther and the Reformation.

A. Bibliographies and Guides to Research

Atkinson, James. "Luther Studies." *Journal of Ecclesiastical History* 23 (1972): 69-77.

Bainton, Roland, and Gritsch, Eric W., eds. *Bibliography of the Continental Reformation: Materials Available in English.* 2nd ed. Hamden, Conn.: Shoe String, 1973.

Bigane, Jack, and Hagen, Kenneth. *Annotated Bibliography of Luther Studies, 1967-1976.* St. Louis: Center for Reformation Research, 1977.

Klug, Eugene F. "Word and Scripture in Luther Studies since World War II." *Trinity Journal* 5 (1984): 3-46.

Lindberg, Carter. "Luther Research in America, 1945-1965." *Lutheran World* 13 (1966): 291-302.

Ozment, Steven E., ed. *Reformation Europe: A Guide to Research.* St. Louis: Center for Reformation Research, 1982.

Pesch, Otto H. "Twenty Years of Catholic Luther Research." *Lutheran World* 13 (1966): 302-316.

Peterson, Brent O. "'Workers of the World Unite—for God's Sake!': Recent Luther Scholarship in the German Democratic Republic." In James D. Tracy, *Luther and the Modern State in Germany.* 16th-Century Studies Essays. No. 7. Kirksville, Mo.: 16th-Century Publishers, 1986.

Robbert, George S. "A Checklist of Luther's Writings in English." *Concordia Theological Monthly* 36 (December 1965): 772-791: *Concordia Theological Monthly* 41 (April 1970): 214-220; *Concordia Journal* 4 (March 1978): 73-77.

The Sixteenth-Century Journal (an annual publication).

Spitz, Lewis W. "Current Accents in Luther Study: 1960-1967." *Theological Studies* 28 (1966): 302-316.

Tjernagel, Neelak S. *The Lutheran Confessions: A Harmony and Resource Book.* Mankato, Minn.: Evangelical Lutheran Synod, 1979.

B. General Works on the Reformation

Bainton, Roland. *The Reformation of the Sixteenth Century.* Boston: Beacon, 1952, 1985.

Chadwick, Owen. *The Reformation.* Pelican History of the Church series. New York: Penguin, 1964.

Dickens, A. G. *Reformation and Society in Sixteenth-Century Europe.* History of European Civilization Library. New York: Harcourt, Brace Jovanovich, 1966.

Elton, G. R., ed. *The New Cambridge Modern History.* Vol. 2. The Reformation. Cambridge: 1958.

Grimm, Harold J. *The Reformation Era: 1500-1650.* 2nd ed. New York: Macmillan, 1973.

Ozment, Steven. *The Age of Reform, 1250-1550: An Intellectual and Religious History of Late Medieval and Reformation Europe.* New Haven: Yale University, 1980.

Pauck, Wilhelm. *The Heritage of the Reformation.* Glencoe, Ill.: Free Press, 1961.

Pelikan, Jaroslav. *The Christian Tradition: A History of the Development of Doctrine.* Vol. 4. *Reformation of Church and Dogma (1300-1700).* Chicago: University of Chicago, 1984.

Spitz, Lewis W. *The Protestant Reformation, 1517-1559.* The Rise of Modern Europe series. New York: Harper and Row, 1985.

Spitz, Lewis W. *Renaissance and Reformation.* 2 vols. St. Louis: Concordia, 1971, 1980.

C. Luther Biographical Studies

Bainton, Ronald H. *Here I Stand: A Life of Martin Luther.* Nashville: Abingdon, 1950, 1978.

Boehmer, Heinrich. *Road to Reformation: Martin Luther to the Year 1521.* Philadelphia: Muhlenberg, 1946.

Bornkamm, Heinrich. *Luther in Mid-Career, 1521-1530.* Philadelphia: Fortress, 1983.

Brecht, Martin. *Martin Luther: His Road to Reformation, 1483-1521.* Philadelphia: Fortress, 1985.

Edwards, Mark U. *Luther and the False Brethren.* Stanford: Stanford University, 1975.

Edwards, Mark U. *Luther's Last Battles: Politics and Polemics, 1531-1546.* Ithaca, N.Y.: Cornell University, 1983.

Erikson, Erik H. *Young Man Luther,* New York: Norton, 1962.

Gritsch, Eric W. *Martin—God's Court Jester: Luther in Retrospect.* Philadelphia: Fortress, 1983.

Haile, H. G. *Luther: An Experiment in Biography* (Garden City, N.Y.: Doubleday, 1980).

Oberman, Heiko A. *Luther: Man Between God and the Devil.* New Haven: Yale University, 1986.

Oliver, Daniel. *The Trial of Luther.* St. Louis: Concordia, 1979.

Osborne, John. *Luther.* New York: New American Library, 1963.

Rupp, E. Gordon. *Luther's Progress to the Diet of Worms.* Chicago: Wilcox and Follet, 1951.

Schweibert, E. G. *Luther and His Times: The Reformation from a New Perspective,* St. Louis: Concordia, 1950.

Siggins, Ian. *Luther and His Mother.* Philadelphia: Fortress, 1981.

Todd, John. *Luther: A Life.* New York: Crossroad, 1982.

Von Loewenich, Walther. *Martin Luther: The Man and His Work.* Minneapolis: Augsburg, 1986.

II. Reference materials on church/state separation.

Bellah, Robert N. and Phillip E. Hammond, *Varieties of Civil Religion* (New York: Harper and Row, 1980).

Church & State, monthly magazine (Available from Americans United for Separation of Church and State, 8120 Fenton Street, Silver Spring, Maryland 20910).

Dawson, Joseph Martin, *America's Way in Church, State, and Society* (New York: Macmillan Co., 1953).

Ericson, Edward L., *American Freedom and the Radical Right* (New York: Frederick Ungar Publishing Co., 1982).

Giamatti, A. Bartlett, "A Liberal Education and the New Coercion," Freshman Address, Yale University, August 31, 1981.

Hatfield, Mark O., *Conflict and Conscience* (Waco, Texas: Word Books, 1971).

Liberty, bimonthly magazine (Available from Review and Herald Publishing Association, 6856 Eastern Avenue, N.W., Washington, D.C. 20012)

Marty, Martin, *Church-State Separation in America: the Tradition Nobody Knows,* a discussion paper, 1982 (Available from People for the American Way).

Richey, Russell E. and Donald G. Jones, editors, *American Civil Religion* (New York: Harper and Row, 1974).

Shriver, Peggy L., *The Bible Vote* (New York: The Pilgrim Press, 1981).

Radical Right Literature

Falwell, Jerry, *Listen, America!* (Garden City, N.Y.: Doubleday and Co., 1980).

Falwell, Jerry, editor, *The Fundamentalist Phenomenon: The Resurgence of Conservative Christianity* (Garden City, N.Y.: Doubleday-Galilee, 1981).

LaHaye, Tim, *The Battle for the Mind* (Old Tappan, N.J.: Fleming H. Revell Company, 1980).

Marshall, Peter and David Manuel, *The Light and the Glory* (Old Tappan, N.J.: Fleming H. Revell Company, 1977).

Walton, Rus, *One Nation Under God* (Washington, D.C.: Third Century Publishers, 1975).

Wood, James E., Jr., et al., *Church and State in Scripture, History, and Constitutional Law* (Waco, Texas: Baylor University Press, 1958).

III. Reference materials on theological disputes.

Bellah, Robert N. *The Broken Covenant* (New York: Seabury, 1975).

Bellah, Robert N. and Phillip E. Hammond, *Varieties of Civil Religion* (New York: Harper and Row, 1980).

The Christian Century, weekly periodical (Available from 407 S. Dearborn St., Chicago, Illinois 60605).

Democracy, "Religion and Democracy" issue, April 1982.

Ericson, Edward L., *American Freedom and the Radical Right* (New York: Frederick Ungar Publishing Co., 1982).

Evangelical Review, quarterly magazine (Available from Cross Roads Publications, 4814 Highway 78, Lilburn, Georgia 30247).

Radical Religion, quarterly journal (Available from P.O. Box 9164, Berkeley, California 94709).

Hill, Samuel S. and Dennis E. Owen, *The New Religious Political Right in America* (Nashville, Tennessee: Abingdon, 1982).

Richey, Russell E. and Donald G. Jones, *American Civil Religion* (New York: Harper and Row, 1974).

Sojourners, monthly magazine (Available from 1309 L Street, N.W., Washington, D.C. 20005).

Radical Right Literature

Falwell, Jerry, *The Fundamentalist Phenomenon: The Resurgence of Conservative Christianity* (Garden City, N.Y.: Doubleday and Company, 1981).

Life's Answer, monthly magazine (Available from James Robison Evangelistic Association, 1801 W. Euless Blvd., Euless, Texas 76039).

Walton, Rus, *FACS! Fundamentals for American Christians* (Nyack, N.Y.: Parson Publishing, 1979).

IV. Reference materials on religious intolerance.

Belth, Nathan C., *A Promise to Keep: The American Encounter with Anti-Semitism* (New York: New York Times Books, 1979).

Blitzer, Wolf, "The Christian Right—Friend or Foe?" *The National Jewish Monthly,* April 1981.

"Concerning Evangelicals and Jews," *Christianity Today,* April 24, 1981, pp. 577-80.

Dart, John, "Israel Finding Born-Again Friends in U.S.," *The Los Angeles Times,* June 11, 1978.

Daum, Annette, *Assault on the Bill of Rights: The Jewish Stake* (Union of American Hebrew Congregations, 1982).

Dialogue, "The New Right: Implications for American Jewry," Spring 1981, pp. 4-14.

Dobkowski, Dr. Michael N., *The Tarnished Dream: The Basis of American Anti-Semitism* (Westport, Connecticut: Greenwood Press, 1979).

Flannery, Edward H., *The Anguish of the Jews* (New York: Macmillan and Co., 1965).

Forster, Arnold and Benjamin R. Epstein, *The New Anti-Semitism* (New York: McGraw-Hill, 1974).

Glock, Charles Y. and Rodney Start, *Christian Beliefs and Anti-Semitism* (New York: Harper and Row, 1979).

Handlin, Oscar and Mary Handlin, *Danger in Discord* (Anti-Defamation League brochure).

Saperstein, Rabbi David, Commission on Social Action of Reform Judaism, *The Challenge of the Religious Right: A Jewish Response,* 1981 (Available for $7.75 from Commission on Social Action of Reform Judaism, 2027 Massachusetts Avenue, N.W., Washington, D.C. 20036).

Radical Right Literature

Grimstead, William, editor, Committee for Truth in History, *The Six Million Reconsidered* (Sausalito, California: The Noontide Press, 1979).

The Spotlight (Available from the Liberty Lobby, 300 Independence Avenue, S.E., Washington, D.C. 20003.)

Varange, Ulick, pseud. (Francis Parker Yockey), *Imperium: The Philosophy and History of Politics* (Sausalito, California: The Noontide Press, 1969).

V. Reference materials on religion and education.

American Federation of Teachers, "The $5 Billion Mistake: Tuition Tax Credits" (Available from AFT, 11 Dupont Circle, N.W., Washington, D.C. 20036).

Anderson, Bill, "Public Schools Are Under Fire, But We Have Just Begun to Fight," *American School Board Journal,* September 1981.

Augenblick, John, "Tuition Tax Credits: Federal Legislation" (Denver, Colorado: Education Commission of the States, *Issuegram,* April 1981).

Bryant, Gene, "Entanglement by the New Right," *Tennessee Teacher,* April 1980.

Lester, Julius, "Moral Education," *Democracy,* April 1982, pp. 28-38.

Lines, Patricia M., *Religious and Moral Values in Public Schools: A Constitutional Analysis,* 1981 (Available for $2 from the Law and Education Center, Education Commission of the States, Suite 300, 1860 Lincoln Street, Denver, Colorado 80295. Report LEC-1).

National Education Association, Connecticut Education Association, The Council on Interracial Books for Children, *Violence, The Ku Klux Klan and the Struggle for Equality,* 1981.

National Education Association, *The Right-to-Work Revival. . . Far Right and Dead Wrong,* 1981.

Park, J. Charles, "Preachers, Politics and the Public Education: A Review of Right-Wing Pressures Against Public Schooling in America," *Phi Beta Kappan,* May 1980.

Raywid, Maryann, *The Ax-Grinders, Critics of Our Public Schools* (New York: Macmillan and Co., 1962).

"Why Public Schools Fail," *Newsweek,* April 20, 1981.

Radical Right Literature

Carle, Erica, *The Hate Factory* (Milwaukee, Wisconsin: Erica Carle Foundation, 1974) Available from P.O. Box 4357, Milwaukee, Wisconsin 53210).

LaHaye, Tim, *The Battle for the Family* (Old Tappan, N.J.: Fleming H. Revell Co., 1982).

—————, *The Battle for the Mind,* (Old Tappan, N.J.: Fleming H. Revell Co., 1980).

Marshner, Connaught, *Blackboard Tyranny* (Westport, Connecticut: Arlington House, 1979).

McGraw, Onalee, *Family Choice in Education: The New Imperative* (Washington, D.C.: The Heritage Foundation, 1978).

—————, *Secular Humanism and the Schools: The Issue Whose Time Has Come* (Washington, D.C.: The Heritage Foundation, 1976).

Morris, Barbara M., *Change Agents in the Schools: Destroy Your Children, Betray Your Country* (Upland, California: The Barbara M. Morris Report, 1979).

Norris, Murray, *Weep for Your Children* (Available from Christian Family Renewal and Valley Christian University, Box 73, Clovis, California 93613, 209-291-4958).

Schlafly, Phyllis, "How and Why I Taught My Children To Read," *The Phyllis Schlafly Report,* June 1981.

—————, "Parents' and Pupils' Rights in Education," *The Phyllis Schlafly Report,* October 1981.

West, E. G., *Critical Issues: The Economics of Education Tax Credits* (Washington, D.C: The Heritage Foundation, 1981).

VI. Reference materials on religion and the courts.

American Bar Association, "Report to the House of Delegates," Special Committee on Coordination of Federal Judicial Improvements, Edward I. Cutler, Chairman, August 1981.

American Judicature Society, *Judicature,* "Limiting Federal Court Jurisdiction: Can Congress Do It? Should Congress Do It?" Vol. 65, No. 4, October 1981.

Cox, Archibald, "Don't Overrule the Court," *Newsweek,* September 28, 1981.

Ericson, Edward L., *American Freedom and the Radical Right* (New York: Frederick Ungar Publishing Co., 1982).

House Judiciary Committee hearings, "Prayer in Public Schools and Buildings—Federal Court Jurisdiction," [Serial No. 63] July 29, 30, August 19, 21, and September 9, 1980.

Kaufman, Irving R., "Congress v. The Court," *The New York Times Magazine,* September 20, 1981.

Leadership Conference on Civil Rights, "Without Justice: A Report on the Conduct of the Justice Department and Civil Rights in 1981-1982," February 15, 1982.

People for the American Way, "The Crusade Against the Courts: An Attack on Our Constitutional Rights," special report, April 1982 (Available upon request).

Senate Subcommittee on the Constitution, "Constitutional Restraints on the Judiciary," hearings of May 20-21, 1981.

Trippett, Frank, "Trying to Trim the U.S. Courts," *Time,* September 28, 1981, pp. 93-4.

U.S. Department of Justice, "The Civil Rights Policy of the Department of Justice: A Response to the Report of the Leadership Conference on Civil Rights," April 3, 1982.

Radical Right Literature

Holt, Earl P., III, "The Supreme Court vs. the Constitution," *Human Events,* November 28, 1981, pp. 10-12.

McGuigan, Patrick B. and Randall R. Rader, *A Blueprint for Judicial Reform* (Washington, D.C.: The Free Congress Research and Education Foundation, 1981).

National Association for Neighborhood Schools, Inc. (Cleveland, Ohio) newsletter.

Walton, Rus, *FAC-Sheet No. 19,* ''Justice & the Courts'' (The Plymouth Rock Foundation, P.O. Box 425, Marlborough, NH 03455).